Mastering the LSAT

The student's guide to success

By veteran LSAT instructor Steve Schwartz

CONTENTS

INTRODUCTION

My LSAT story

I have been coaching the LSAT for over 10 years. I originally wanted to be a lawyer and was targeting the top 14 law schools, but I got sidetracked and found myself obsessed with the LSAT. I never did go to law school, but I've found my calling running a test prep company – LSAT Unplugged – as well as the related YouTube channel and podcast.

I went to an Ivy League school for my undergraduate degree, so getting a 152 for my first LSAT score was a bit of a surprise, to say the least. It took me a whole year to crack the code and get a score of 175. Once I did, I thought to myself, "Hallelujah! I want to spread the word!" Friends from high school and college started asking me for help with their test prep and things snowballed from there. After graduating from college, I started teaching the LSAT full-time and haven't looked back since.

I specialize in coaching students who want to improve their scores, overcome test anxiety, and master the LSAT. I've been through the process and climbed my way from a perfectly average score to the 99th percentile. The good news is that I put 98% of my material out there for free. I have released countless hours of free material on the LSAT Unplugged YouTube channel and podcast, and I've authored over 1,000 articles on every element of LSAT preparation through my website. I have in-depth study regimens and schedules that are unlike those supplied by the big prep companies. I also record my one-on-one coaching sessions with students so you can directly experience what it's like to work with me and gain new insights along the way.

This book is an easy-to-use summary of everything I've learned in my years of living and breathing the LSAT. I break down how to master every LSAT question type, share my best study strategies, and take you step-by-step through test day and beyond.

What is the LSAT?

The Law School Admission Test (LSAT) is used to determine if a student has the skills necessary for success in law school because it's correlated with first-year law school grades. The LSAT is graded on a scale of 120 to 180, with 120 being the lowest possible score and 180 being the highest possible score. The median score is around 151, which means half of the test-takers scored higher and half scored lower.

The LSAT has three scored sections: Analytical Reasoning section (aka Logic Games), one Logical Reasoning section, and one Reading Comprehension section. Logic Games are short puzzles, somewhat mathematical-seeming in nature. Logical Reasoning is comprised of brief bite-sized arguments. Reading Comprehension may look like something from the SAT, but it's actually looking for you to analyze arguments presented, rather than absorbing the information itself.

A fourth unscored and undisclosed experimental section is also included, which I'll cover in more detail later. For now, know that it will typically be one of the three major section-types (Logic Games, Logical Reasoning, or Reading Comprehension.) And finally, there is an unscored Writing Sample administered separately.

Ultimately, the LSAT is designed to assess two major abilities: short-term working memory and critical reasoning skills. In other words, the test-makers want to gauge your ability to properly examine, evaluate, and analyze arguments.

If you're looking for more detail beyond what I share in this book, my LSAT courses include in-depth explanations of each section and question type.

(And if you think the LSAT doesn't test anything important, you'll soon find out that these are skills you'll use in law school, when you will be evaluating real legal cases and real-life scenarios that are more similar to LSAT-style questions than might seem obvious at first glance.)

Why take the LSAT?

The LSAT has been in existence since 1948 and has evolved through many formats over the years. However, the current major question-types (Logic Games, Logical Reasoning, and Reading Comprehension) have remained largely the same since 1991 (despite a few minor changes, such as the addition of the dual Reading Comprehension passages in June 2007, which I discuss later).

The LSAT is significantly harder than the GRE, GMAT, MCAT, SAT, ACT, etc. It's unlike anything you learned in school. It doesn't test math or vocabulary. Rather, it puts your critical thinking skills and short-term working memory to the test. Oftentimes, students are in for a rude awakening when they first encounter the LSAT, but it can be conquered in the end.

The LSAT is considered a valid and reliable admission test because it has a strong correlation with first-year law school grades. Interpreting arguments on the LSAT is highly similar to interpreting fact patterns in law school. On the LSAT, there are ambiguities in the fact patterns. The job of the test taker is to spot these ambiguities and identify the gap in reasoning between the evidence and the claims conclusion. This skill is crucial for both law students and attorneys working in our often-ambiguous legal system.

The LSAT is designed to test your ability to read carefully and in detail. As an attorney, a small word change or even a comma can radically change the meaning of a document, which could have a significant impact on a client.

Because the LSAT is so challenging, improving your LSAT score requires a lot of hard work. However, getting the highest possible LSAT score will dramatically improve your chances of getting into the best law school and minimizing your debt load with scholarship money. Some of my students have even gotten full rides to law school (paying nothing in tuition) along with living stipends. Yes, you can actually get paid to go to law school! The key is to achieve an LSAT score above the median to the school to which you're applying. Why would schools offer such generous scholarships? Because it raises their status in the U.S. News rankings.

When to take the LSAT

If you plan on going to law school immediately after undergrad, you'll want to apply to law school during your senior year of college. Ideally, you should take the LSAT in the spring of your junior year.

If you're a junior now, you might want to take the LSAT in March or April so you have the option to retake it in June or July if needed. Then you can apply to law schools at the very beginning of the cycle in September, which would be the fall of your senior year. If you're currently a senior, I hope you've already started studying! You can take the test in November or January and then apply immediately after you get your score.

The LSAT is offered in cycles (roughly aligned with the school year) and you can retake it during each cycle. Law school deadlines vary from school to school and can be lenient and flexible in certain cases. But the longer you wait to apply the harder it will be to get in and the smaller the pool of available scholarship money.

If you're taking the LSAT after January, I would typically suggest waiting until the next cycle to apply. That means if you're taking the LSAT in February, you would wait until the fall to apply for a start date one year later. Ideally, you would apply right when applications open in the fall to maximize your chances and available scholarship money.

On average, the earlier you apply, the better your odds. However, it can be worth waiting a bit to retake the LSAT if you can raise your score. After all, LSAT scores are the biggest factor in admissions, and even one point makes a difference. For example, if you need to retake the LSAT in November, you could apply after you get your new score and not be at a significant disadvantage. There's still plenty of scholarship money available, and your chances of getting in are still high. A short, strategic delay could lead to thousands of dollars more in scholarship money or getting into a better law school. It's the easiest money you'll ever make, period.

What happens if your retake score is lower than the previous one? No big deal. It happens. Sure, it's better to improve on a retake, but law schools in the U.S. only consider your highest scores in the admissions process anyway. Why? Because they have an incentive to do so. The U.S. News rankings that are so important to admission officers are based on the LSATs and GPAs of matriculating students. If you can help them raise their median LSAT score, then they have reason to want you (and give you scholarship money). They'll record your best and ignore the rest.

What skills are required?

The LSAT doesn't test legal knowledge; it tests critical reasoning. It has a lot more to do with philosophy and formal logic than law itself because it's testing a way of thinking. This is important to know, as it affects how you should prepare.

Learning formal logic is like learning to speak a new language, which we call "legalese." Additionally, a lot of achieving a top score on the LSAT comes down to having a critical and skeptical mindset. You have to evaluate arguments as they are written without inserting your own assumptions or expectations. Many times, upon reviewing a problem with a student, we go back to the actual text and ask, "What does the question actually say?" You always want to be asking: "How or why is evidence true? How is the given information valid?" It is not always a valid conclusion, meaning the conclusion is not guaranteed to follow from the evidence provided. It's possible for the evidence to be true yet for the conclusion to be false.

Let's say that a restaurant has a five-star rating on Yelp. Despite this, you don't want to go there. How is it possible that you wouldn't want to go to a restaurant even though it has a five-star rating? (Assuming that five stars is the highest possible rating.)

How could all of the previous statements be true? Well, there are actually several factors that could help to explain this potentially confusing scenario (on the LSAT, they might call this an "apparent discrepancy"). Maybe the ratings are fake. Maybe they only have one review. Maybe you don't like the cuisine, or the restaurant is not conveniently located. There are a lot of reasons you might not want to eat at a highly-rated restaurant. In other words, the conclusion does not automatically follow from the evidence.

There's a strategy for everything you might encounter on the LSAT. But my LSAT strategies are not only about helping you master logical thinking. Why? Because it's not just about getting the questions right. It's about getting them right under timed test day conditions.

After a brief aside to discuss how the LSAT relates to law school admissions, the GRE, and prep for college freshmen, I'll show you the specific skills needed to successfully complete Logic Games, Logical Reasoning, and Reading Comprehension questions.

Next, we'll work on cultivating the right mindset. This includes test-taking strategies like pacing, endurance, time management, and the process of elimination. I show my students how to relax and increase their confidence, so they can focus on what they need to do on Test Day.

Most LSAT prep books underemphasize Test Day preparation. Since 2005, I've been working on training my students to simulate test-day conditions and overcome any anxiety or nerves. This is essential because LSAT questions feature complex arguments about topics you are probably not familiar with. It takes a certain level of reasoning and engagement to break down these questions and make them relatable. This is all about the right mindset, and it's a skill that can be developed over time.

Here's an example of a bizarre LSAT question that challenges conventional thinking and assumptions. The question involves a doctor who is a smoker and wants to ban smoking in public places. Now, this is strange for a variety of reasons. First off, we don't expect doctors to be smokers. They are supposed to be healthy and we expect them to lead by example! But of course, in reality, there are countless exceptions to this rule.

Additionally, this smoker (who just happens to be a doctor)wants to ban smoking in public places. Why would a smoker want to ban smoking? Once again, this example challenges our preconceived notions and biases, leading students astray. I train my students to focus only on the logic of the question and set aside their personal assumptions, even under the stress of Test Day itself.

THE LSAT AND LAW SCHOOL ADMISSIONS

Law school admission process

Beyond the LSAT, it pays to start the entire law school application process earlier than you think you need to. That involves requesting letters of recommendation from professors or employers and starting to work on your personal statement, any optional essays, and your resume. It's a long process.

It's also wise to apply to more law schools than you think you might need to. Some people only apply to three or four schools, and they're really limiting themselves. In all honesty, 10 or 12 schools are not too many. You can use a scholarship offer from one school to negotiate more money at another. Plus, your plans could change. Some schools offer part-time programs, and some offer joint degrees. You want to maximize and consider all options .

To help strategize the list of schools to which you'll be applying, you can look at the published LSAT and GPA medians of the previous matriculating class at the schools you're targeting. These numbers are available online. You can check out the LSAC website to find data to help you asses your chance at getting into a particular school.

I have hundreds of free articles on my website that provide application advice, personal statement samples, and much more. While the LSAT is the most important factor, there are many other elements that can make or break a law school application.

The LSAT vs. the GRE

If someone has strengths in certain areas, are they better off taking the GRE? UCLA Law School Dean of Admissions Rob Schwartz says that less than 5% of their admitted students have only a GRE score. In short, it's not a major focus. Even though many law schools have started taking the GRE, the LSAT is still the main game in town.

Why consider GRE scores at all? Many law schools accept them in order to attract STEM majors who are reluctant to take the LSAT or who have already taken the GRE anyway. If you're a STEM major, schools definitely want you, because STEM combined with law is a killer combination. Schools want to produce lawyers who can understand intellectual property law, patents and trade, trademarks, drugs and medical products, and more. However, schools still want LSAT scores that can help them boost their U.S. News ranking.

In short, you can take the GRE if it appeals to you, but you're probably not doing yourself any favors by skipping the LSAT.

LSAT preparation for college freshmen

If you are a college freshman, you shouldn't worry too much about studying actual LSAT material yet, because you still have your entire undergraduate GPA ahead of you. Rather, focus on building strong study habits to help you get the highest undergraduate GPA possible, and start reading some books on formal and informal logic. Consider taking a general philosophy class to acquaint yourself with difficult, dense text, as these courses often include texts similar to what you'll read on the LSAT. Enjoy college first and foremost, but get your GPA up and keep it as high as possible.

Then, in sophomore or junior year, if you still intend to go to law school, get your hands on a few LSAT books and books on informal logic. I like the book

A Rulebook for Arguments by Anthony Weston. It's very similar to *The Elements of Style* by Strunk and White, which is a concise guide to grammar. It's a rulebook that will acquaint you with the different types of arguments and flaws you'll see on the LSAT. If you read that and are still interested in law school, get all the old LSAT exams (LSAC's LawHub is the best source since the LSAT is online) and start working through them using the LASER approach, which I will outline later in this book.

If you get stuck, don't worry. Check out my website, YouTube channel, and podcast for free resources that supplement this book. I've created resources in all formats to demystify any question type could possibly stump you.

THE LSAT SECTIONS

And how to approach them

There are three different scored sections on the LSAT: Logic Games, Logical Reasoning, and Reading Comprehension. This chapter will focus on the content of each, including how to study and the habits of top scorers.

Logic Games

The Logic Games section, (also known as the Analytical Reasoning or Puzzles section) is the most loved and hated part of the LSAT. After all, most people haven't done anything like this before!

Sure, Logic Games can be challenging, but the glory of triumph, when you make a huge inference at the start of a game is not much different from finding the area where a particular jigsaw puzzle piece fits. Because making big inferences is all you really need to do here (rather than understand a detailed argument), this section is the easiest to learn and perfect.

If the fact that they're called "games" isn't enough to convince you that they can be fun, keep in mind that they're similar to sudoku and crossword puzzles (each bit of progress you make builds on a previous part). In fact, it's not a huge leap to say that they use the same part of your brain.

Each section of Logic Games contains anywhere from 22-24 questions, divided among 4 separate groups or "games." Each game has anywhere from 5-7 questions. While Logic Games do not follow a strict order of difficulty within a section, the first game tends to be easier than the fourth.

Because each Logic Game section is 35 minutes, this means that you should devote an average of eight minutes, 45 seconds per game. However, this is only an average. If you intend to complete all 4 Logic Games (as most test-takers realistically shooting for a 160+ score should), you will most likely spend less time on at least one of the Logic Games and more time on another.

All Logic Games begin with a prompt presented in a short paragraph. The prompt is followed by a list of indented rules (or limits) based upon that prompt. The game then has anywhere from 5-7 questions associated with the prompt and a list of rules.

Types of Logic Games

In increasing order of difficulty, most Logic Games fall into three major categories: Ordering, Grouping, and combinations of both game types. More detail on these games can be found in the Logic Games section later in this chapter.

ORDERING GAMES

Ordering games are the most basic game type. You're given a list of variables (letters) to place in a particular order. This order will typically result from the game's chronological nature, (putting variables in order because they occur one after another) or because they're ranked (tallest to shortest, biggest to smallest, etc.).

GROUPING GAMES

There are three main types: In-Out / Selection, Splitting, and Matching.

- **In-Out / Selection:** Your job is to divide the variables into separate groups, "In" and "Out." The task is to select some variables, but not others.

- **Splitting:** Your job is to divide the variables into separate groups, both of which are present. These groups could be "1" and "2," or two letters, like "R" and "S."

- **Matching:** Your job is to associate variables of one type with variables of another type. For example, scholars might be matched with the languages that they learn. Notice that there is no sequencing aspect in this game. The scholars are not learning the languages in any particular order, nor are they ranked.

COMBINATION GAMES

Combination games tend to be noticeably more difficult because they contain elements of multiple basic game types.

Habits of top scorers

They diagram.
Lesson: Organize the information contained in each game's initial paragraph and rules.

They are able to adapt to new situations (games that seem unfamiliar).
Lesson: Be flexible and use the information the game gives you in the most efficient way possible. Recognize that the nature of various games can differ, and use the limitations to create an appropriate diagram.

They have good short-term memories.
Lesson: Learn to hold the basic rules and setup in your head while applying rule changes and specific limitations.

Logic Games format

All Logic Games begin with a scenario approximately five lines long. The scenario is followed by a list of indented rules (or limits), based upon that scenario. The game then has anywhere from five to seven questions associated with the scenario and list of rules.

Logic Games approach in a nutshell:

- Read scenario.
- Identify game type and create the main diagram.
- Diagram rules.
- Make connections between the rules (known as inferences or deductions).
- Answer questions.

Reading the scenario first allows you to identify the game type and create a main diagram to represent it.

While learning and identifying game types isn't necessary, it can be helpful. Why? Because it makes it a bit easier to relate a new game to games you've previously done. I find that many of the best test-takers are able to solve new games efficiently because they have a mental framework for sets of rules and tasks that the game asks them to perform. Diagram each piece of information in the game's initial paragraph as you read it. Why create a diagram? It's useful to have a picture of what's going on in the game because it lets you see everything at once. Symbols take less time to read and write than tiny words do. Creating a diagram allows you to save time.

You might say, "But creating a diagram wastes time! I could be using that time to solve the questions." On the contrary, it's virtually impossible to hold the entire game in your head at once. Even if you could, why go to the trouble when a diagram will save you a lot of work?

After taking the time to make a diagram, look at the rules (the conditions referred to in the scenario). Just as I've recommended diagramming the scenario, I also recommend diagramming the rules. Whenever possible, it's useful to create symbols to make your information appear in a more concise form. Symbols take less time to read and write than tiny words do. This will simplify your handling of the game. when you need to remember the rules at lightning speed and apply them to the questions. You'll want to diagram each rule as you read it, but it's also important to look back at previous rules after you read a new rule. This will help you make inferences.

Making inferences is the best technique to quickly complete Logic Games.

Inferences are like rules, only they're rules that the LSAT doesn't give you directly. They're deductions you figure out on your own. You determine them by connecting pieces of information the LSAT gives you with each other. Since the questions in Logic Games often require you to make inferences, you're going to want to make those inferences at some point or another during the game. This gives you two main options:

1. You can make these inferences on the spot for each particular question on an as-needed basis.
2. You can make these inferences at the beginning of the game, as you're initially diagramming the rules before you even move on to the questions.

I recommend #2 whenever possible.

Sure, properly setting up a Logic Game and making all the inferences and deductions associated with the rules can take time. In some games, it can take up to 3-4 minutes to set up the game and make all the inferences. This is about 1/3 of the average 8 minutes and 45 seconds you have per game.

STEVE SCHWARTZ

However, **the payoff for doing this work up-front can be huge**. If you make all the inferences and deductions yourself before approaching the questions, you'll be able to solve the questions more efficiently, and you'll be able to enjoy the benefit of all that work over the course of the game. This can save you a lot of time, allowing you to blast through the questions in less than a minute each in some cases.

Finally, you'll want to answer the questions (which is really the whole point of everything we've done so far).

Common questions associated with Logic Games

Orientation questions

These questions ask you to choose the answer choice that contains a valid or acceptable scenario or "list" of variables in compliance with the rules. Four of the answer choices will violate at least one of the rules, one answer choice will not violate any of the rules.

Example: "Which one of the following could be the order in which the cars are parked, from one to six?"

There are two ways to approach this type of question: one is inefficient, and the other is efficient.

1. The inefficient way

Look at the first choice and test all the rules and inferences against it. If it choices this way until you find a choice that does not violate a rule.

Why is this inefficient? Because it requires you to constantly cycle through all the rules as you review each choice.

16

2. The efficient way

Take one rule or inference at a time and check through all five answer choices to determine which do not comply with it. Eliminate those that do not comply. This is what I consider to be the "assembly-line method" of attacking this question-type. It's more efficient and you still get the right answer, only you get it more quickly.

Typically, you can expect to eliminate a maximum of one or two answer choices with each rule, but it's still worth going through the other answer choices to check them for compliance with that rule just in case.

Sometimes you'll find that a particular rule can be used to eliminate more than one or two answer choices.

Inferences often result from the combination of multiple different rules. This means that in a game with a major inference, it's more efficient to apply that inference to all five choices rather than to apply a straightforward given rule to all five choices. You'll often find that applying an inference to each answer choice will eliminate multiple answer choices, allowing you to arrive at the correct answer more quickly.

General "Must" and "Could" questions

(You don't necessarily have to memorize the following info, but you do have to understand it. If understanding it requires that you memorize it, memorize it.)

"Which one of the following statements must be true?"

(Equivalent to "Each of the following statements could be false EXCEPT" and "Which one of the following statements cannot be false?")

4 of the answer choices don't have to be true. Each of the wrong answer choices might only happen in some cases, or it's possible that some wrong answer

choices might not ever occur. In any case, they could be false. The correct answer choice is the one that must be true for all valid scenarios. It would not be possible to create a scenario where the correct answer choice did not occur.

"Which one of the following statements could be true?"

(Equivalent to "Each of the following statements must be false EXCEPT")

Four of the answer choices can't be true for any valid scenario. The correct answer choice can occur in at least one valid scenario.

"Each of the following statements must be true EXCEPT"

(Equivalent to "Which one of the following statements could be false?")

Four of the answer choices must be true for every valid scenario. The correct answer choice does not always have to occur.

"Each of the following statements could be true EXCEPT"

(Equivalent to "Which one of the following statements must be false?" and "Which one of the following statements cannot be true?")

Four of the answer choices could (or must) occur in some valid scenario. The correct answer choice cannot occur in any valid scenario.

"If" / specific

"If" questions impose new limitations on the game's possibilities, by providing additional information. In other words, these questions impose a further limitation on the game's possibilities aside from the initial rules. It's important to recognize that this question's limitation is not fundamentally changing the rules of the game. Rather, it's simply further restricting (for the duration of this question only) the possibilities that were already present. Any valid scenario resulting from this question is still a valid scenario for the game as a whole.

You may find that diagrams you've previously drawn in the past (or chosen as the correct answer from the Orientation question) will be sufficient to solve this question, or to at least eliminate an answer choice or two. If you haven't yet created a diagram containing the information in the "if" question, it's time to draw a new diagram.

Take the information provided by the question and combine it with what you already know to determine how this new information affects the possibilities. The limitation provided by the question will generally allow you to determine a good deal about the placement of the variables. It might not allow you to determine the placement of every single variable, but this is fine. You don't always need to know where every single variable goes. You simply need to apply the new limitation and determine its impact.

Part of doing well on Logic Games is being comfortable with uncertainty and recognizing that you might not always have a completed diagram. You simply need to combine the rules with the new limitation. You always have enough information to answer the question. Note that any of the previously-mentioned general "Must" and "Could" questions, could be turned into an "If" question simply by adding a statement like, "If G is in slot 3" or "If G is selected" to the beginning of the question.

Example:

General version: "Which one of the following statements must be true?"

"If"/ Specific version: "If G is selected, which one of the following statements must be true?"

Words and characteristics to help you to recognize each game type:

Ordering games use the words: before, after, sequentially, in order, chronologically and contain: numbers, times, days of the week.

Typical rules:

- "A is before B."
- "C is after B."
- "D is immediately before E."
- "G is immediately after F."
- "The 5th space is always occupied by either G or F."
- "H always occupies either the first space or the last space."

Examples:
- A monkey eats 6 M&Ms, but no two M&Ms are eaten consecutively.
- A kid performs 7 songs, one song per day.
- A judge ranks 8 performers in a competition.

Common tasks:
- Which variable(s) must be placed in a particular spot?
- Which variable(s) cannot be placed in a specific spot?
- Which variables must be consecutive (adjacent)?
- Which variables cannot be consecutive (adjacent)?
- How many spots must there be between two variables?
- How many spots can't there be between two variables?
- Which variables must occur before or after each other?

Grouping games use the words: if/then and contain: conditional rules and/or links between different types of variables.

Typical rules:
- "If A is present, then B is not present."
- "If A is in group 1, then B is in group 2."
- "If C is not present, then B must be present."
- "A is always associated with B."

- "C is never associated with B."
- "B is always associated with at least two other variables."

Examples:
- A monkey chooses to eat some M&Ms, but not others (In-Out).
- A kid performs some songs today and the rest tomorrow (Splitting).
- A judge decides which performers advance to the next level in a competition (In-Out).
- A monkey places each M&M with a banana (Matching).
- A kid decides which instrument(s) are used to perform a variety of songs (Matching)
- A judge places 8 performers into 3 different categories (matching).

Common tasks:
- Which variable(s) must be selected (in)?
- Which variable(s) cannot be selected?
- Which variables' selection requires other variables to be selected (or not selected)?
- Which variables' absence requires other variables to be selected (or not selected)?
- Which variables must be together?
- Which variables cannot be together?
- Which variables must be in a particular group?
- Which variables cannot be in a particular group?
- Which variables require other variables be (or not be) in a particular group?

Combination games can be identified by the fact that they contain rules that fall into multiple categories, rather than only one.

Logic Games strategies

You will learn to pinpoint problem sections in Logic Games by going back to the fundamentals, checking the rules of the game, and making sure you've correctly diagrammed everything. **A symbolic note-taking strategy can also work for you.** I recommend using all capital letters for the variables and making sure that everything is as neat and clean as possible. It's very easy to mistake one letter for another sometimes, and then it all falls apart. I've also found that making charts simply doesn't work for me. I prefer to write out all the rules and create slots. If you'd like to see examples, I have free video explanations on my YouTube channel for the vast majority of Logic Games.

Logic Games are all about timing. If your technique doesn't get you to the correct answer fast enough, then it's not really serving you. You need to blast through the easier games to build up a time bank for the tougher games that come later. There's also a strategy to the order in which you use the questions. If you're running out of time, skip the hard question and make sure you answer the easy ones. Working with games, means holding general principles in your head, as you go through the game drawing, making local diagrams. As such, if there is a game where you don't see as much upfront work, don't panic. It's probably not new. It could just be the game itself holding you back.

Discerning among many hypotheticals to eliminate answer choices is an acquired skill. You'll notice some of the newer games (starting with PrepTest 57 and up to the present) often include a rule substitution or rule equivalency question. In context, it can seem like a curveball, because you have to totally re-conceptualize the game. Drill idea:why not practice all the rule substitution questions in isolation from every exam? In other words, do just that question from each game. This will help you see the patterns in how to solve them, and allow you to develop a strategy.

Some quick advice on "rule sub" questions: if a given answer choice renders a previously valid scenario invalid, then it could not possibly be true because it's more limiting. If you allow scenarios that would not normally be allowed, it's less limiting, and therefore can't be equivalent. The correct answer is going to link that answer choice with the other rules.

Studying means repetition, so you aren't seeing something for the first time on test day. If you've done five or six games of a certain type, ideally you'll be able to breeze through an easy one of that type in five or six minutes, then have time to tackle the tougher questions later.

And this is why I would never recommend timing yourself with the 8-minute and 45-second constraint for any particular game in isolation. Instead, I would suggest doing the games as a set of four per timed section. Then you can benchmark where you are. Game one might take 10 minutes, game two might take seven minutes, and so on.

Once you are aware of the timing, you can then look to reduce it. Something like the famous CDs game featured in Legally Blonde (PrepTest 31, Game 2), is most certainly going to be a 12-minute game for most people looking at it for the first time. The idea is to familiarize yourself with these games as best you can and get better at the easier games that come earlier in the section. As a result, you are building up a "time bank" to apply later to the tougher ones.

The biggest thing is to look for is games that repeat, so you can solidify your understanding of the concept. Some could be identical to each other in virtually every important way. You draw your contrapositive, link your conditionals together, and take it from there. But a tougher "curveball" game may requiring a bit more flexibility in approach. It's fine if those take longer.

It's also important to recognize when you're getting bogged down. You don't want to get stuck in "quicksand" at the expense of missing out on an easier game that comes later. You don't have to get them all, but you do want to attempt every single one. If you feel yourself getting stuck, just guess, flag it, and move on. Ideally, you'll have time to come back to it later. And don't over-complicate diagramming more than you really need to (I've seen students develop crazy systems involving circles, triangles, and squares!)

Some of the weirder curveball games require adaptation and flexibility. You have to get your head around whatever tricky situation they throw at you. The unfortunate thing about weird curveball games is that they're not even that similar to one another. At LSATUnplugged.com, I have a list of every curveball game that's ever appeared on the exam. They're really valuable to review once you've mastered the easy games.

Logical Reasoning

This section contains short, bite-sized arguments where you have to perform tasks like strengthening the argument, weakening it, or identifying its conclusion or major flaw.

The Logical Reasoning section can feel like the most complicated part of the LSAT because it has the greatest number of question-types. It contains complex methods of reasoning, so it requires you to understand detailed arguments. Logical Reasoning sections typically contain anywhere from 24-26 questions. They're also clearly placed in a general order of difficulty - they get progressively harder as the section goes on. Because each Logical Reasoning section is 35 minutes, this means you should devote an average of about 1 minute and a half to each question. However, this is only an average. Since there's an order of difficulty, you'll want to spend less time on the easier questions, and more time on the tougher questions.

All Logical Reasoning questions begin with a prompt presented in a short paragraph, called the stimulus. This typically contains an argument of some kind, or, if not that, a set of facts. The stimulus is then followed by a question stem - a question that asks you to interpret the reasoning or facts in the stimulus in some way.

Just about everyone loves to complete Logical Reasoning questions by category based upon their question stem (the question following each short paragraph). To a certain extent, this makes sense, as you have to understand what the question is asking in order to solve it. Drilling by **question-stem** type can help you solidify your understanding of what sort of information the question is specifically asking for. However, a more practical reason for discussing questions by question-stem type is simply that it's easy to categorize questions by their question stem. You can do this without taking the time to actually read the stimulus.

Since your ability to solve LSAT Logical Reasoning questions will be greatly enhanced by gaining an understanding of the principles underlying Logical Reasoning stimuli (the short paragraphs preceding each question stem), let's take some time to focus on the stimulus' method of reasoning- more specifically, the gap between evidence and conclusion. This allows us to engage with each question on a deeper level.

By focusing on Logical Reasoning questions based upon the method of reasoning in the stimulus, you'll get a better understanding of the argument. This, in turn, puts you in a better position to answer whatever particular question-stem LSAC throws at you related to a particular stimulus.

When reading a stimulus, we should first determine **whether it contains an argument or a fact set.** We can do this by searching for a conclusion within the stimulus.

Fact sets are a group of sentences that don't contain a conclusion. As such, they're not trying to convince us of anything. You can't really disagree with the validity of the set of statements as a whole, since there isn't a statement that is not attempting to support another. The following is a fact set:

> "Keisha has brown hair. Janice has blonde hair. Georgette has purple hair. Hair is a filamentous biomaterial that grows from follicles found in the dermis." (I borrowed the final sentence from Wikipedia).

These sentences are dull and boring, and it's not just because the final sentence is kind of science-y. It's hard to get passionate about these statements or disagree with them since they don't contain any kind of reasoning, opinion, or conclusion - just hard facts.

However, **in arguments**, certain statements support others. The statements giving support are our evidence (also known as our "premises"), and the statement or statements receiving support make up our conclusion(s).

We can think of the conclusion as being the opinion of the person "speaking" in the stimulus. The following is an argument:

> "All celebrities have had problems with alcohol and/or drugs. Lindsay Lohan is a celebrity. Therefore, she's had problems with alcohol and/or drugs."

The author's purpose in providing us with the first two statements is to convince us of this final sentence, so the final sentence is our conclusion. The preceding two sentences serve as the author's evidence for the conclusion and serve as the argument's premises.

This argument happens to be perfectly valid, leaving no gap between the evidence and conclusion. If Lindsay is a celebrity, and all celebrities have these types of problems, then Lindsay must have these types of problems as well. There's no gap between the evidence and conclusion in this case. The author of these statements happens to have provided us with sufficient (enough) evidence to completely support the conclusion, leaving no ambiguity or doubt about the conclusion. Whether the first two sentences are actually true or not, is completely irrelevant for our purposes on the LSAT - they are our "givens", so we simply have to assume that they are true. The validity of the argument does not depend upon the truth of the given statements - only whether the given statements are sufficient to support the conclusion being advanced by the author of the argument. In other words, we don't have to concern ourselves with defining "celebrity" or investigating whether it's actually true that all celebrities have had problems with alcohol or drugs—although it would certainly seem that way from reading the tabloids or watching "E!"

Note: you could restate the above no-gap argument as the following:

Evidence #1: A requires B
Evidence #2: B requires C
Conclusion: A requires C

This is an airtight argument—it can't be strengthened or weakened, because the evidence 100% justifies the conclusion. The two evidence statements can be connected to form a longer chain (A requires B requires C), leaving no ambiguity about the conclusion's validity.

However, in most LSAT arguments, the evidence does not fully support the conclusion. In other words, there will usually be some kind of gap between the evidence and the conclusion. The gap can be described as the underlying assumptions that the argument requires in order to be true.

Here's an example of an argument containing a big gap:

"While at a bar, Jane asked John to watch her bag while she went to the bathroom. When she returned, both John and her bag were gone.

Therefore, John must have stolen her bag."

While it's understandable why the author of this argument believes that John stole Jane's bag, this is not the only possible explanation. To conclude that this is the only possible explanation would be to assume that no other potential explanations could make sense. What are some other potential explanations?

Here are a few:

1. John met someone else and left with them, forgetting all about Jane's bag, and Jane's bag was stolen by someone else.
2. John turned his back for a moment and Jane's bag was stolen by someone else. John feared Jane's wrath at his negligence, so he panicked and fled.
3. John had an emergency and had to leave suddenly, but he didn't want someone else to take Jane's bag, so he took it with him.

The author of this argument has failed to consider that any of these alternative explanations might be possible or correct. As such, the argument makes a big leap of logic by jumping to the conclusion that John stole her bag. We can say that this argument is flawed.

However, some arguments contain small gaps. In these cases, while the evidence still does not fully support the conclusion, it better supports the conclusion than in those cases with big gaps in reasoning.

Had the conclusion been milder, saying something like, "Therefore, John probably stole her bag," the argument would be stronger because its claim is less extreme, and it's easier to support a more moderate conclusion. The more extreme or definitive the conclusion, the more difficult it is to support.

Again, there are plenty of things we don't know, like John's relationship with Jane, or his trustworthiness, so we can't say how likely it is that he stole her bag. However, because this version of the argument is not as extreme, its assumptions are more moderate, so the gap between the evidence and the conclusion is smaller. It requires less of a leap.

So, how do we judge whether an argument contains a big gap or a small gap? This is where our reasoning abilities come into play. Part of engaging with the stimulus requires evaluating how reasonable it is.

Fortunately, however, the LSAT isn't asking us to determine whether the gap between the evidence and conclusion is big or small. It's simply asking us about the nature of the gap itself.

- If the argument is viewed as containing a **big gap**: what the argument is failing to consider.
- If the argument is viewed as containing a **small gap**: what the argument is failing (or just not bothering) to explicitly state.

Accusing the argument of failing to consider something is to place the blame on the individual making the argument. In other words, the question assumes that the person making the argument didn't even realize the assumption he or she was making.

On the other hand, when the LSAT asks us to point out something the argument failed to explicitly state, it allows for the possibility, that the person making the argument recognizes this assumption and just didn't bother to mention it.

Types of arguments

- **Fact sets** (somewhat common on the LSAT) are likely to be associated with Inference questions: Must Be True, Most Strongly Supported, and Cannot Be True.

- **No gap arguments** (rare on the LSAT) are also likely to be associated with Inference questions (again, Must Be True, Most Strongly Supported, and Cannot Be True)

- **Small gap arguments** (common) are often associated with Strengthen, Weaken, Necessary Assumption, and Sufficient Assumption questions.

- **Big gap arguments** (common) are often associated with Flaw questions.

Logical Reasoning

1. Identify question type by reading the question stem.
2. Find whether the stimulus contains fact sets or arguments.
3. If fact set, try to make connections between parts.
4. If argument, determine reasonability of argument.
5. Try to pre-phrase answer based on question-type. Alternatively, start by eliminating wrong answer choices.

Types of Logical Reasoning questions

Most Logical Reasoning questions fall into 2 major categories: Questions where the information in the stimulus is assumed to be true and the information in the answer choices are under suspicion, or questions where the information in the answer choices is assumed to be true and the information in the stimulus is under suspicion.

Let's start with the first category:

Questions where the information in the stimulus is assumed to be true and the information in the answer choices are questionable. The stimulus is a given, while only one of the answer choices (the correct one), is "true." Your task is to determine which of them is true, given the information in the stimulus.

(Focusing on the major question-types for now.)

INFERENCE

- Must Be True
- Most Strongly Supported
- Main Conclusion / Complete Argument
- Necessary Assumption
- Flaw
- Parallel Reasoning
- Point of Issue
- Method of Reasoning
- Role of Statement

Now, let's look at the second category:

Questions where the information in the answer choices is assumed to be true, and the information in the stimulus is considered questionable. All five of the answer choices are assumed to be "true," and the stimulus is problematic in some way. Your task is to determine which of the answers will have a particular impact on the stimulus.

- Sufficient Assumption
- Strengthen
- Weaken
- Resolve the Paradox

The question-type commonly referred to as "Principle" questions have the potential to be either - it really depends upon other aspects of the question-stem, so I'm not including them here.

Let's briefly look at each of these in a little bit more detail, starting with these inference questions:

INFERENCE

- *Must Be True*
- *Most Strongly Supported*
- *Main Conclusion / Complete the Argument*

Must Be True: Your job is to select the answer choice that needs to be 100% true, without any doubt, based upon the information in the stimulus.

Most Strongly Supported: Your job is to select the answer choice that is very likely to be true, but doesn't necessarily need to be guaranteed 100%.

Main Conclusion / Complete the Argument:
Your job is to select the answer choice that best describes the argument's primary goal- its main point.

- **How to ID:** "must be true", "most strongly supported", "cannot be true", "logically follows", "properly inferred"
- **Sample Question Stem:** "If the statements above are true, which one of the following must also be true?"
- **Approach:** Look for connections in stimulus. If nothing jumps out in choices, use process of elimination. If multiple conditionals, create formal logic diagram.

Let's look at other question-types where the stimulus guarantees one of the answer choices:

- Necessary Assumption
- Flaw
- Parallel Reasoning / Parallel Flaw
- Point at Issue
- Method of Reasoning
- Role of Statement

Necessary Assumption: Your job is to select the answer choice that needs to be true in order for the argument to work.

- How to ID: "assumption" with words "depends upon", "requires", "assumes", "presupposes"
- Sample Question Stem: "Which one of the following is an assumption upon which the argument depends?"
- Approach: Negate each choice. Correct choice, when negated, destroys argument's validity.

Flaw: Your job is to select the answer choice that identifies the argument's error in reasoning.

- **How to ID:** "flaw", "error", "vulnerable to criticism", "questionable", "fallacious", "unwarranted", "weakness"
- **Sample Question Stem:** "The argument is vulnerable to criticism on the grounds that it"
- **Approach:** Determine mistake in method of reasoning without looking at choices, then find description in choices.

Parallel Reasoning / Parallel Flaw: Your job is to select the answer choice that contains the most similar method of reasoning to that in the stimulus.

- **How to ID:** "most closely parallel to", "most similar to", "logical structure", "pattern of reasoning"
- **Sample Question Stem:** "Which one of the following arguments is most similar in its reasoning to the argument above?"

- **Approach:** Determine method of reasoning or flaw in stimulus. Articulate abstract version of method of reasoning, search for similarity in choices.

If there are multiple conditionals, create formal logic diagram.

Point at Issue: Your job is to determine the issue on which the two people disagree.

- **How to ID:** 2 people in stimulus with "disagree over" or "point at issue between"
- **Sample Question Stem:** "The dialogue lends the most support to the claim that Jenkins and Lurano disagree on whether..."
- **Approach:** Find choice which both people express opinions on, and expressed opinions are in opposition to one another - 1 person says "yes", other says "no."

Method of Reasoning: Your job is to determine how the stimulus goes about making its argument - what sort of evidence is used to support its conclusion.

- **How to ID:** "method of reasoning", "argument proceeds by", "responds...by", "employs...strategies/techniques"
- **Sample Question Stem:** "The argument employs which one of the following reasoning techniques?"
- **Approach:** Determine type of evidence used to support argument's conclusion.

Role of Statement: Your job is to determine the function of a particular part of the argument.

- **How to ID:** "plays which one of the following roles", "figures in the argument"
- **Sample question Stem:** "The claim that inventors sometimes serve as their own engineers plays which one of the following roles in the argument?"
- **Approach:** Identify parts of argument in stimulus to determine how the

statement fits in.

Now, let's look at question-types where the answer choice will have a particular impact on the stimulus.

- Sufficient Assumption
- Strengthen
- Weaken
- Resolve the Paradox

Sufficient Assumption: Your job is to guarantee the argument's validity, leaving no ambiguity at all - you ensure that the conclusion logically follows from the stimulus.

- **How to ID:** "assumption" with words "allows", "enables", "follows logically / properly inferred...if assumed"
- **Sample Question Stem:** "The conclusion above follows logically if which one of the following is assumed?"
- **Approach:** Guarantees conclusion's validity by linking evidence with conclusion.

Strengthen: Your job is to support the argument's conclusion.

- **How to ID:** "strengthen", "most strongly supports", "most justifies", "most helps to justify", "additional support"
- **Sample Question Stem:** "Which one of the following, if true, most helps to strengthen the argument?"
- **Approach:** Make conclusion more likely to be valid.

Weaken: Your job is to undermine the argument's conclusion.

- **How to ID:** "weaken", "call into question", "strongest logical counter", "undermine", "cast doubt", "incomplete"
- **Sample Question Stem:** "Which one of the following, if true, most seriously undermines the conclusion above?"

- **Approach:** Make conclusion less likely to be valid.

Resolve the Paradox: Your job is to reconcile seemingly inconsistent statements - to explain how these facts could both be true.

- **How to ID:** "helps to resolve/reconcile" "apparent/seeming paradox/ discrepancy/ inconsistency/ contradiction", "contributes to an explanation"
- **Sample Question Stem:** "Which one of the following, if true, most helps to resolve the apparent discrepancy above?"
- **Approach:** Look for the choice that points out a way for everything in stimulus to be true at same time.

Habits of top scorers

They don't simply take claims (conclusions) at face value.
Lesson: Be critical and skeptical of arguments.

They recognize that while evidence is true, the conclusion may not be true.
Lesson: Consider potential alternative causes for any result and potential alternative explanations for any conclusion.

They devote obsessive attention to detail, understand nuances, and apply general principles to specific situations.
Lesson: Do the same. Don't skim!

Reading Comprehension

Now that we've covered Logic Games and Logical Reasoning in-depth, let's discuss the oft-neglected Reading Comprehension section. One reason this section is neglected by both prep companies and students is that many feel they don't need to study for it -- reason being there are sections of the same name on the SAT and ACT. However, it's actually quite different from these sections of the same name. On the LSAT, Reading Comprehension tests your ability to understand the structure of passage and the intent of the author, rather than any sort of substantive knowledge. The Reading Comprehension section may be the most difficult part of the LSAT to improve upon, even if it may seem more familiar than the other sections at first glance.

The Reading Comprehension section contains anywhere from 26-28 questions, divided into four different groups, with no obvious order of difficulty. These four groups consist of three long passages and a pair of two short ones, known as dual passages or comparative reading. The two short passages are labeled Passage A and Passage B. They're grouped together and are on related topics. In PrepTests prior to June 2007, there were simply 4 long passages. (In case you were wondering, this is why you'll see 4 long passages within each RC section in PrepTests 1-51.)

For all passages, topics cover a broad range: humanities, science, social science, and law/politics. Because each RC section is 35 minutes, this means you should devote an average of about 8 minutes and 45 seconds for each of the 3 long passages, and 8:45 (in total) for the two dual passages as well. However, this is only an average. You'll want to spend less time on the easier passages and more time on the tougher ones. Each of the 3 long Reading Comp passages is about 450 words, and the dual passages are each about half that length (200-250 words). You might think of each RC passage as being like a big Logical Reasoning stimulus, and the associated questions being analogous to the questions you'd see in Logical Reasoning. Although these sections might appear very different on the surface, there are many similarities.

Just as with Logical Reasoning, LSAC pulls from a limited set of topics. And, as with Logical Reasoning, the topic is not particularly important, since the LSAT does not require outside knowledge.

Examples of humanities topics that have appeared:
- Objectivism vs. subjectivism when studying the mind
- Latin texts in Renaissance England
- Authoritarian rulers and democratic reforms/change
- Victorian philanthropy

Examples of law topics that have appeared:
- Criminal procedure systems—adversarial vs. inquisitorial
- Defense lawyers' obligations and innocence/guilt of clients
- Email privacy and the law
- Legal systems in US vs. England

Examples of natural science topics that have appeared:
- Recombinant DNA (rDNA)
- Serotonin and carbohydrate cravings
- Neurogenesis and canaries
- Dinosaur extinction, volcanic-eruption theory vs. impact theory

Examples of social science topics that have appeared:
- Psychology of decision-making and risk-taking
- Steady-state economics vs. neoclassical economics
- The law and literature movement
- Political attitudes / institutions in England vs. American colonies

Examples of minorities/women topics that have appeared:
- Personal names in Hopi (Native American) culture
- Korean Americans, cultural identity, and the Pico Korea Union
- African American communism in Alabama
- Women's participation in the French Revolution

Types of Questions

Many Logical Reasoning questions have a parallel type in Reading Comprehension. Fortunately, the strategies for those questions apply to Reading Comp as well. Of course, Reading Comp contains a few types of questions you won't see in Logical Reasoning such as "what is the author's attitude?" The "must be true" questions are often trickier as well.

Guiding questions

Keep the following questions in mind as you look at the relationship between the evidence and conclusion throughout the passage.

What evidence is given in each paragraph?

- What kind of support do the advocates of each stated position provide? Do the viewpoints follow from this evidence?
- To what extent does the evidence justify the viewpoints stated in the passage?
- Are the viewpoints well-supported, or is there some doubt as to whether they really do?

Does the passage author promote any guiding principles?

- Not every viewpoint is necessarily a hard and fast conclusion like in Logical Reasoning, where A is stated to cause B, for example. Principles may appear a bit more nuanced, as general theories or hypotheses that the author isn't 100% sure about.

Does the passage describe any counter-arguments?

- Does the passage discuss multiple viewpoints? Are they at odds with each other? On what points do they agree or disagree? What evidence is presented to strengthen or weaken them?

Does the author agree or disagree with any counter-arguments?

- Does the author acknowledge the shortcomings of the dominant viewpoint (whether it's described neutrally or is the author's personal opinion), or is the author more firmly in favor of / uncritical of the dominant viewpoint?

What is the author's tone, and how does it change over the course of the passage?

- Is the author critical and biased, taking a strong stance or opinion? Or is the author more balanced? Does the author take any position at all, or is he/she more neutral? Does the author start off neutral, then express an opinion later in the passage? Is the author cautiously optimistic, skeptical, and limited in the extent to which he/she favors one viewpoint, or does the author wholeheartedly argue in favor of one side over the other?

What is the role of each example in the argument?

- What purpose does each particular statement serve in the overall argument presented at that particular point in the passage? Your goal as an active reader is to constantly be looking at the role of each statement in the argument as a whole—like a big Logical Reasoning role-of-the-statement question.

What is the purpose of each paragraph in the passage, and what is the overall passage's argument / goal?

- Why does the author say this at all, and why does the author say this at this particular point in time? When you walk away from the passage after you've finished reading it, you should be able to communicate the passage's main idea—the primary viewpoint presented, and the author's purpose, or reason, for writing the passage at all in the first place. Ask yourself—if you could walk away from the passage with only one piece of information, one idea, what would that idea be?

Main Idea / Main Point / Central Idea:

Approach: Look for the author's viewpoint, or whichever viewpoint gets more attention in the passage. Answer must be true of entire passage, not only one part of it.

Most of the time, these questions ask about the author's viewpoint or whichever viewpoint is given more attention and space in the passage.

It's the author's conclusion. Approach main point questions just as you would approach Logical Reasoning main point / conclusion questions. The main point is NOT the summary. It's simply what the authors are trying to convince you is true. This will most closely resemble an opinion, rather than background info or undeniable facts. It can be at the beginning, middle, or end.

But it's often the aspect of the topic covered in the majority of the passage, not only in one paragraph. LSAT-takers often fall for choices that describe specific parts of the passage, rather than the majority of the passage.

Depending upon the type of passage, the main point will take different forms.

If the passage is about a:
- problem, the main point is the solution.
- mystery (cause / effect), the main point should be the explanation the author advocates.
- person the author likes / dislikes, the main point is that the person is great / not great. Evidence will be reasons for opinion.
- study / experiment, the main point is that the study / experiment is good / bad. Evidence will strengthen / weaken study's validity by attacking study / people conducting it.

Consider doing these questions first since they're the easiest. Solving them will also help you articulate the passage's overall argument for yourself.

Specific/Detail Questions:

Approach: Don't look too deeply into the choices here. Look for a paraphrase of information in the passage.

Inference Questions:

Approach: Remember specific portions of the passage, or find explicit justification within the passage, before selecting a choice.

They don't actually ask for new information. They'll often require you to take the contrapositive of something in the passage or to simply connect different parts of what's already there. This means you simply have to read a little deeper into relevant lines of the passage. Reading "between the lines" can obviously be difficult to do, but there's a common "trick" LSAC often uses in more difficult RC inference questions.

For these questions, the passage gives you the information you need (as it does for all inference questions). However, the passage simply presents this info in a way that makes it difficult to see and extract this info. In other words, this information is presented indirectly. The passage tells you something the author (or a person within the passage) doesn't believe. As a result, if you read carefully, you will indirectly learn about what the author (or person within the passage) does believe.

These questions may also ask you to make a prediction based upon the argument. If they do, examine the structure of the passage and note the various points of view within. Go back to areas where the author summarizes the tone and argument. Whenever the question refers to a certain piece of evidence or particular line, analyze its role in the argument. Look a couple of lines above and below it.

Meaning-In-Context Questions:

Approach: Read above and below the referenced portion of passage, possibly even much earlier or much later in it, to find the contextual meaning of this phrase.

Strengthen / Weaken:

Approach: Consider new information's impact on the likelihood of the argument's validity.

Primary Purpose / Function:

Approach: Similar to main idea but choices use more abstract language. Evaluate verbs used in each choice.

These questions are very similar to main point questions. The difference? The answer choices are more vague; in other words, they use more abstract language. Pay very close attention to the verbs used in each answer choice.

Role of Statement Questions:

Approach: Use contextual clues to determine how statement plays a role in the author's overall argument.

Author's Attitude:

Approach: Look for indications of author's opinion throughout the passage, particularly adjectives.

Passage Organization:

Approach: Use process of elimination, checking each answer choice against notes on passage's structure.

Parallel Reasoning:

Approach: Form generalized version of topic in question and find the answer choice that best fits it.

Real-world (outside) topic knowledge

Outside knowledge helps because it gives you familiarity with the passage's subject. This can prevent you from "falling asleep" and can help you distinguish between the viewpoints.

Outside knowledge hurts because you can't use it to answer the questions. Don't let it distract you!

* Read quickly, but don't skim.

What do I mean by this?

When most people think of skimming, they think of reading on a superficial level. They try silly strategies like reading the first and last sentence of each paragraph. Hey, if it worked for grammar school textbooks and the SAT, it'll work here, right?

Wrong.

LSAT Reading Comp passages are organized differently than in textbooks (or SAT passages), and they have a different focus.

You want to read quickly, but you don't want to skip the middle of a paragraph just because it's the middle. The LSAT often includes important nuggets in the middle of passages because people tend to gloss over them.

Read slightly slower than a typical skim, but faster than a thorough read.

You're not reading for content or facts. Instead, you're reading for argumentative structure and for the positions and viewpoints presented.

The bottom line: don't try to absorb all the content. Reading for structure means that you should focus on certain types of information, but not others. You should focus on the positions advanced by the author, and read this information more slowly. When you see the details, the evidence, the author presents, read more quickly.

If you take note of the structure, you'll know where to find each nugget of information in the passage when the questions ask for it. In short:

- **DO** mark-up the passage quickly and efficiently, reading for structure and arguments.

- **DON'T** focus on details and examples, underlining and highlighting half the passage.

I know LSAT Reading Comprehension passages can be difficult. They throw a bunch of information at you all at once. For this reason, it's natural to want to do something to keep track of it all. So, since it is possible to take notes, to underline, to highlight, to circle things, you want to know which of those things to do. And, of course, LSAT companies can't sell books or teach classes without having something to teach in them, so they come up with strategies that will fill the books and take up class time.

Now, if you find that taking notes actually helps you, that's great—do it. However, taking notes is not for everyone. I find that the students who do best on Reading Comprehension mark very little, or not even at all. Personally, I don't take notes at all. I leave the passage blank. If you're not the kind of person who likes taking notes, there's no reason to start now. However, I understand that some students *do* like to take notes. If you do, consider the strategy I lay out in the next section. It's a simple, minimal marking system that doesn't take a lot of time and keeps you focused on the passage's structure. However, like I said, even I don't use it - I don't make any markings at all.

For any Reading Comprehension note-taking strategy you use, take the time to rigorously test whether it's actually helping you. If it's not helping you, there's no reason to do it, because it's costing you time, right?

Your notes are useful if they help you:
- remember what you marked;
- identify key parts of the passage;
- answer the questions; and
- understand the passage.

Your notes aren't useful if they:

- don't help you remember key details;
- don't help you answer the questions;
- take too much time to make;
- take up too much space; and
- leave out parts of the passage's structure.

Complete a couple of Reading Comprehension sections with your current note-taking strategy, then complete a few sections without taking any notes. Then try a different strategy. Compare the results, see which is associated with the best results, then adopt that strategy. (And keep in mind that different note-taking systems work for different people. It's not a one-size-fits-all kind of thing.)

At the end of the day, it's ultimately about understanding the passage and remembering the key viewpoints and structure as you go forward to answer the questions. Then, you need to be able to hunt through the passage for the specific details you need as quickly as possible, in order to answer detail-oriented questions.

A simple note-taking strategy

Although taking notes can keep you focused, the fewer notes you take, the better. Why? Because it costs time, just as making overly-complicated diagrams on Logic Games does.

Consider pausing while you read to write a short note every now and again. **Instead of focusing on content, try to understand the passage's flow / structure as well as the author's intent.** The details aren't as important as the main idea. It's more important to know where in the passage to find the details and unfamiliar terms, than it is to know *what* they actually mean during your initial read of the passage.

Try not to spend too much time focusing on keywords—this will likely slow you down and interrupt your concentration. However, it's useful for you to note people or groups mentioned in the passage because there are often questions about them.

You'll develop your note-taking technique as you complete more passages and learn to recognize the most important details of each passage. Refine your approach to underlining and note-taking over time. As you practice, you will be able to decrease your dependence upon this method as you learn which pieces of info are most important. **And remember, ultimately, we want to focus on understanding a passage's structure, not the details.** Aside from reducing your stress ("do I really have to understand everything on my initial read?!"), this will keep you focused on what truly matters when it comes to solving the questions associated with the passage. After all, the test-makers don't actually care about the passage's topic.

"Wait a moment," you ask. "Could that really be true?!"

Yes -- it's actually true. The test-makers don't care whether you can become an expert on a random topic in just a few stressful minutes on a timed LSAT exam. But they do care if you can absorb the method of reasoning, i.e. the underlying principles of an argument in a short amount of time.

What this means for you: don't try to memorize all the details in the passage. Don't fall into the trap of getting bogged down on your initial read of the passage; try to spend maximum 3 minutes.

Instead, focus more on understanding the passage's main idea and primary purpose. This allows you more time to solve the questions associated with the passage afterwards.

Habits of top scorers

They keep track of various opinions presented by individuals or groups.

Lesson: do the same. Don't skim!

They stay within the information provided in the passage.

Lesson: Be able to support each inference with a specific line reference in the passage.

They focus on structure, not content.

Lesson: Analyze each paragraph as if it were a Logical Reasoning stimulus.

Reading Comprehension Format

Two big format changes in recent years involve locating text references and the new "passage only" view. These features are unique to the online LSAT Reading Comp section; they were not available with the paper version. On LSAC's LawHub platform (as on ProctorU during Test Day itself), there are no longer line number references. (On the paper exam, the lines are numbered every five lines to give you a reference point. For instance, they'll say, "In line 36, the word antidisetablishmentarianism means what in this context?") Figuring out the meaning and context for particular vocabulary words used to involve going back to a particular numbered line reference.

There are no longer any line references because the online LSAT allows test-takers to increase and decrease the text size, which makes the text somewhat fluid. It's not fixed in space, like it would be on a piece of paper, so the line numberings will change as you change the text size. LSAC wanted to remove any ambiguity or confusion, so instead they highlight the words in the question stem, and they highlight that specific text in the passage to give you a quick reference. The color they use for highlighting that text is aqua green / blue, unlike the three colors you have access to for your own highlighting: yellow, pink, and orange. As for a question-solving strategy, just go immediately to that particular part of the passage they're referencing and read for context a few lines above and below.

As for the "passage only" view vs having passage and questions side by side, personally, I prefer the latter. However, it's worth your time to experiment and see what works for you. As I've said, Reading Comprehension, more than any other section, is personal in nature.

How to Increase Reading Speed

You can't overcome an entire lifetime of never reading books and then suddenly attack Reading Comprehension on a standardized test like the LSAT. It could take several months to build this skill.

As depressing as that may sound, I have good news for you. If you'd like to speed up, there are many strategies that can help you in the short term.

In particular, I'd recommend that you start by reading publications like Scientific American or The Economist online, just to practice reading dense, difficult text at greater and greater speeds.

Phrasereader.com allows you to copy and paste text and display it at various speeds. You can also narrow your field of vision to individual chunks of text so you can't see the entire thing at once. This tool is very desktop-friendly, so you can copy and paste in pretty much anything.

Spreeder.com is also great, and is more app-friendly. You can use free public domain text from Project Gutenberg, and even PDFs of the old LSAT exams if you have them. I recommend copying and pasting the text from them into these apps or using the aforementioned magazine and newspaper. You want dense text that's tougher than the average listicle or email you're typically used to reading on a screen.

How to study the sections

I would never time individual Logic Games or individual Reading Comprehension passages, because they vary in difficulty. But as a whole, games and passages typically go from easy to harder within each section. It's typically best to work through easier questions more quickly to build up a time bank you can use later on the tougher questions.

When you first begin studying, I suggest starting with Logic Games. It's the most difficult, but also the easiest to improve upon. Once you gain a basic familiarity with Logic Games, then introduce Logical Reasoning (while still staying fresh on Games). Finally, mix in Reading Comprehension while still doing a bit of Games and Reasoning on the side.

In short, focus on one, but still keep mixing in the others here and there. I wouldn't do only once section at the exclusion of the others. You can also rotate between them, depending on if you get exhausted or tired of one section. Ultimately, I don't think it matters too much which one you focus on, or when. I like having a primary focus and then a secondary focus to mix it up a little bit, but still keeping a focus on one area, that way you can see the patterns between different question types.

It is possible to improve significantly on the LSAT, especially on the Games section. If you have done no studying at all and start off with a diagnostic score of 140, then you should be able to score in the 150s with just a few months of work. If you're studying well and using high-quality resources and real exams, along with giving yourself ample time each week, you could improve even further. If you've been studying for a few months and have a basic familiarity with all the exam sections, it's best to identify your weak areas and focus on them. After a couple of months, you should do a diagnostic to see where you stand. You can then introduce pacing and endurance into your prep, in addition to accuracy.

Order of approach

In Logic Games, it's best to do orientation questions — the "gimme" questions asking something like, "which one of the following could be a vaild scenario?" — at the beginning, then move onto local "if" questions, then global questions. As you do local questions, you build up a bank of previous valid scenarios of these hypotheticals. You can use this to help you eliminate wrong answers in the global questions.

Use the diagrams related to previous hypothetical scenarios that you've drawn. Too often, students draw diagrams and don't reuse them. But the work you did for question #3 could help you solve question #5, and your correct answer to the orientation question (the first question of the game) will give you a hypothetical to use as well.

For these reasons, you shouldn't necessarily do Logic Games questions in the order given. It's likely that doing an orientation question, then the local, and then global is more efficient than simply doing them in order.

However, in the Reading Comprehension section, it's the opposite. It's often best to do the main point and primary purpose questions first. Other global questions to do first include: passage organization, best title for the passage, best tone of the passage, and author's opinion. Then move on to the detail-oriented questions with references to a specific parts of the passage. End with the inferential questions that involve reading between the lines or asking what the author would be most likely to agree with. Because the questions typically aren't strictly asked in the order mentioned above, I would not recommend always doing the questions for a passage in the order given.

To provide you with some time benchmarks, I would aim to read the passage itself in about two and a half to three minutes. This way, you can spend the remaining time on the questions themselves. If you spend any more than three minutes on your initial reading of the passage, you will have significantly less than one minute per question, because there are generally six or seven questions per passage. As such, if you have, on average, 8:45 per passage, minus three minutes for your initial read, you're already down to 5:45 to answer six or seven questions. You really don't want to go below that!

Logical Reasoning contains short, grab-bag questions with no groupings. There is a general order of difficulty in Logical Reasoning across the entire section. For these reasons, I would simply work through them in the order given. I would not do the hardest Logical Reasoning questions first, as there is no reason to do the harder ones and risk never getting to the easier ones.

(Note: In Logica Reasoning, it's a general order of difficulty, but not a perfect order of difficulty. In fact, the last two or three questions might actually be easier than the ones around 18-22 or 15-22. Typically, I find that 24-26 are usually slightly easier.)

There is also something to be said for the momentum of building confidence as you go, getting more correct as you move on, and then saving the toughest ones for last. Also, by using the online LSAT's "flagging" feature, you can easily skip questions while marking them to come back to later.

I typically flag three or four questions in a single Logical Reasoning section because I simply don't want to deal with them in the moment. I would rather skip them and come back at the end when I at least have the confidence of knowing I have completed this section. This helps me avoid getting stuck in "quicksand" while the clock is ticking.

LSAT writing sample format

The LSAT Writing Sample (aka "LSAT Writing") requires you to assess a situation or dilemma and choose between two options. The goal is to present a strong argument for the option you support and a strong argument against the other, creating a well-balanced case. The exam time limit is 35 minutes, and that restraint is strictly enforced.

I'll now share some information about the testing format before getting into strategies. Just as the LSAT moved from being administered in-person to online, the same is now true of LSAT Writing. It's to be completed at home, or in any quiet environment you'd like. For security reasons, you must be the only one in the room, and you'll be instructed show them with your webcam that no one else is around to help you and no other resources are available.

Unlike on the actual LSAT, LSAC won't monitor you live with someone on the other end watching you during the LSAT Writing. Rather, they'll simply save a recording in case they need to check it for security purposes later. (There are troubleshooting tools on the LSAC website to help you make sure you're doing it properly.) You can complete this section anytime starting 8 calendar days prior to your scheduled LSAT testing week.

Be aware that your may experience technical issues. Something unexpected could affect the webcam or your Internet connection. Your roommate or random papers may be in the background, which could cause LSAC to invalidate the session. This would requie you to redo it and potentially delay the release of your LSAT score. You want nothing in the room that could be an issue, so plan ahead as much as possible and review all related rules on LSAC's website!

However, a major benefit of these changes is that you're now only doing the actual LSAT sections during your exam sitting – Logic Games, Logical Reasoning, and Reading Comprehension – that's it. And you're not obligated to do your writing sample on the same day. However, I recommend not procrastinating. You run the risk of forgetting about it, and LSAC will not release your test scores to you or the law schools until you have completed it. Again: your score will not be released to anyone until you have at least one writing sample on record.

This section is still not scored, but it may weigh a bit more heavily than it did previously in the law school admission process because it's now typed rather than handwritten. Most people's handwriting is terrible these days, because we're not used to writing in cursive anymore. Typing is more legible, so it's easier to read what students have written and evaluate their writing. Law schools may be reviewing these more closely than before, but, quite frankly, that's not saying much, because they hardly paid attention to them in the past. I might devote a little bit more attention to it than previously, but I wouldn't worry too much about it, as the writing sample content has not changed at all.

Since you'll be typing instead of writing by hand, you'll likely work through this section faster, unless you have accessibility issues. This will give you more time to review what you have written. I would suggest that you spend 20-25 minutes on drafting the writing sample, then another 10-15 minutes editing your work, making it as polished as possible. Proofread and check your spelling, punctuation, and grammar. There is a spell-check feature, but it's still worth reading through to double-check everything. Make sure you've done your best possible work. Use the full 35 minutes and take it seriously.

You don't have to study much, if at all, for the writing sample. I would rather you focus significantly more on the scored portions of the LSAT. Note: the writing sample is most important for applicants who are non-native English speakers and those with lower grades in English or writing classes, where there might be a question about the student's English fluency and/or writing ability.

The good news is that once you've completed the writing sample you'll never have to take it again – no matter how many times you take the LSAT. Your writing sample will remain valid for as long as your LSAT score is valid. That said, you do have the option to pay $15 and submit another one. If you previously wrote one and you don't think it reflects your true potential, then it's worth spending an additional $15 to do another that better reflects your ability.

Since it's not part of your scaled LSAT score out of 180, some people treat the writing sample as a joke. **The writing sample does matter, but not nearly as much as the scored sections of the LSAT.**

Experimental Section

As I stated previously, non-native English speakers should give it special attention, because admission officers will want to see if you are proficient in written English. Similarly, if your grades in college English classes were terrible, the writing sample is your chance to show that you are a strong writer and your college grades are not reflective of your true ability. LSAT Writing is the one chance law schools have to see if you truly have the ability to write clearly and persuasively, which is an undoubtedly an important skill on both the bar exam and in the practice of law itself.

A UCLA Law School admissions officer once admitted to me that he only read one out of ten handwritten writing samples in the past. With thousands of applications to review, he (like countless other admission officers) simply didn't have the time to read all the writing samples along with all other application material, especially with potential handwriting issues slowing the review!

Previously, with the paper version of the test, having the writing sample as the last section also made for sloppy writing. Now that you don't have to do the writing sample at the test site, test takers are expected to do a better job on this portion. Are admission officers definitely going to look at it? Not necessarily, but if they do, you want your writing sample to reflect your full effort and ability.

Don't waste your time doing 50 practice writing samples, but doing a few isn't a terrible idea. It will help you feel prepared and know what to expect whenever you choose to complete this section.

Unfortunately, the writing sample is one of those things with a small upside and a big downside. It probably won't get you into law school, but if you do a terrible job it could potentially lead to a rejection. However, if you're already a strong candidate, you give it your full effort, and do satisfactory job on it, you'll be fine.

Why does LSAC even use experimental sections? The purpose is to test new questions for future actual LSAT administrations. Often, the experimental section is just marginally easier or harder than the typical LSAT section, and LSAC is administering the questions to determine how they might need to adjust the difficulty of the section as a whole. The content typically won't differ substantially from what you've seen elsewhere.

However, if at the end of the exam, you had two sections of Logic Games or two sections of Logical Reasoning, you will know that at least one of them was experimental. But you won't know which specific one unless you talk it over with others after the exam and ask, for example, "Did you have a game on flowers?" If the other person didn't no, you know that your game with flowers was experimental and not scored. Other than that, you typically won't know which one was experimental during the exam, so it's important to put forth your best effort in all sections.

STUDY SCHEDULES

What is too much? When is too early? What's not enough? I would recommend allowing a minimum of five to six months to study for the LSAT in order to reach your fullest potential. Most people only want to spend two to three months studying, but that's generally because they underestimate just how difficult and important this exam is.

I probably don't need to explain the LSAT's difficulty, but I'll make a brief mention of its importance here. Each law school (with a few exceptions) publishes its "law school admissions index" on LSAC's website. This formula shows how they consider your LSAT score relative to your undergraduate GPA. The findings? While law schools vary in just how much more heavily they weigh your LSAT score relative to your GPA, almost all weigh it far more heavily.

And, if you've ever looked at an practice LSAT, you already know that you likely have some work ahead of you. Suffice it to say, the LSAT takes commitment. If you have the luxury of planning ahead, it would be best to plan on studying and taking the LSAT in junior or senior year of college, or shortly after if possible. The reason being that it's tough to balance studying for the LSAT with working full-time, possibly living in a new city with a new roommate, fulfilling family obligations, maintaining relationships, etc.

Devoting time to LSAT prep is essential to doing well; there is no way around it. It's ironic how you spend so much time building your GPA, only to have it count for much less than your LSAT score when applying for law school.

You earn your LSAT score in one day, and yet it bears more weight than the GPA you've spent years building.

Treat the LSAT like a 100-credit course, the challenge being, that you likely have only months to study for it instead of years. Although I recommended allowing at least five to six months to prepare, if you are retaking, two to three months should be sufficient. I somehow had the "good fortune" of spending an entire year studying for the LSAT! It's not just about making the time commitment. It's also about creating a smart strategy.

If you have the luxury to study for the LSAT full-time, treat your study like a job or important appointment by blocking off time to make it happen. Create a structured schedule for every single day that you study. One full-day study schedule to use on weekends or days off from work and school might involve studying for about three hours in the morning, then take a break for lunch. Study for another two to three hours, then wrap up for the day. This will give you about five to six solid study hours per day without burning out. Put your study sessions int your calendar as a way of committing to them.

Balance is essential to retaining what you've learned. Structuring your study time into your life helps keep your mental capacity sharp. If you try to commit every waking hour to study, you will stress yourself out and fail to achieve what you set out to do. Your normal schedule will undergo some changes, but you don't have to stop doing everything you're used to doing. Keep time for exercise, mindfulness, meditation, socializing—whatever fills your cup, because you will need this in order to keep your studies going strong.

All of this really makes a difference, because you've got to be at your sharpest for the LSAT. If you're even a little bit off – tired, hung-over, and maybe a little bit rusty because you've spent too much time away from the LSAT – it can have an impact on the results, even if you studied. There are always obstacles and distractions to overcome. If you're married or have kids, you will need support from your partner and family members. If you have a roommate, you need them to understand your study schedule and its importance.

Another strategy to consider is the Pomodoro Technique, which involves studying in cycles that include regular breaks. For example, each half-hour will have a five-minute break. Basically, study for 25 minutes, then take a five-minute break, study for another 25 minutes, take another five-minute break.

Once you've built a strong foundation in the basics of the LSAT, I'd suggest taking one timed exam each week. Ideally, the time of day that you complete it will be the same time of day as your actual exam itself so that Test Day itself feels like just another practice test.

However, don't fall into the trap of doing a timed exam every single day; this is a recipe for burnout. Do at most two timed exams per week, along with a detailed review of those exams. That will be more than enough. If you identify weak areas to focus on, you can drill those on the side. Taking too many practice exams gives you less time to focus on improving your weak spots.

Ideally, you should complete at least 30 to 40 exams altogether before Test Day Some should be individual timed sections, some as individual questions by type, and others as full-length timed exams. Focus on slow and steady progress. When you are studying full-time over the course of five or six months, it's easy to burn out. Make sure you take plenty of breaks during each study session, and take some full days off from studying here and there. Don't feel like you need to do too much on any single day. The LSAT preparation process is a marathon, not a sprint. It's about absorbing the methods of reasoning that the exam tests, and this happens over a long period of time.

Not everyone has the luxury of time on their side, but if you do, I highly advise setting aside enough the time in your calendar to study at a slow and steady pace. In my experience, the students who allow significant time for the material to sink in are the ones who end up with the highest LSAT scores in the end.

You may want to take the LSAT more than once, so your study schedule should account for that. Plan on taking your first LSAT at least a year out for your best chance at getting a top LSAT score. Just to give you an idea, I'm going to include below a quick breakdown of some timelines that would be fine for taking the LSAT and still allow you time to retake, if necessary, and apply with time to spare.

If you take it in October or November to apply for admission for the following fall, that gives you enough time. Even taking it in January and applying to start law school in the fall is not too late. However, if you take the LSAT in the spring, that's quite late if you want to start law school that same year. If you're planning ahead by taking it in February and want to apply that fall to start law school the following fall, that's wonderful, because you're way ahead of the game. That means that you could retake the LSAT in June, with another retake in July, still allowing you the opportunity to apply at the very beginning of the cycle in the fall.

However, the LSAT is offered nearly every month now, so if you initially took the LSAT in October, you could retake it in November and only have to stay fresh for a few weeks instead of months. In this scenario, do one timed exam per week, plus a review of your first exam and the areas for which you felt least prepared. In my opinion, there's no reason to apply to law school with only one LSAT score. It's always worth taking it at least a second or third time because, through luck alone, you could improve significantly.

Even one point on the LSAT could get you into a better law school or earn you significantly more scholarship money. A higher LSAT score could get you $10,000 a year. Over the course of three years, that's a huge amount, especially if it reduces your debt or allows you more career options upon graduating. Your LSAT score could even get you a full ride to law school, meaning that you wouldn't have to pay anything at all to attend. Some of my students have even gotten living stipends in addition to the full ride; in other words, they got paid to go to law school! The time that you spending to study for the LSAT is the best return on investment you'll ever get, especially considering the ripple effect it has over the course of your entire career.

Can you prepare for the LSAT in three months?

It's possible, but that time frame is not ideal. It's almost impossible to reach your fullest potential in three months. You don't necessarily need to reach your fullest potential to go to law school, but higher scores generally mean more options. It might take one student a year to reach their highest potential, but that doesn't mean that the student actually needs to devote a year. A lot of top-scoring students spend six months or more – even up to a year – to achieve scores in the 170s on test day, but that doesn't necessarily mean that it will take you that long.

Another point to consider is that you may not need to achieve a score in the 170s for the schools you want to attend. However, two to three months is still typically not enough time. The LSAT is much harder than other tests you've likely encountered done up to this point, so it's worth investing the time.

Your study plan should include the following stages:

Stage 1: Accuracy – Focus on getting the basics down and getting the questions right.

Stage 2: Pacing – Do timed sections to get into a rhythm, for doing those sets of questions within 35 minutes.

Stage 3: Endurance – Do full-length, four-section, timed exams to build stamina for test day.

These stages take a lot of time. You might spend two or three months just in the accuracy phase. It's a long process – much more than students typically expect – but if you want to qualify for scholarship money and get into better law schools, five to six months (or more) of study and preparation is well worth the investment.

Structured LSAT study schedules

Self-study is an integral part of any LSAT study process. Even if you take a course, it doesn't take the place of self-study. Ultimately, you have to put in the work on your end – and that means putting in the time with actual LSAT PrepTests.

However you approach your LSAT prep, it's worth devoting significant time, even if you feel like you're not progressing at first. Remember that it takes time for things to "click'." A course with a rigorous schedule can help because it breaks down each of the sections and question types, allowing you to build a strong foundation before you take a full timed exam. Without a plan of attack, you will just be spinning your wheels. There are some key elements that all study schedules have in common, but yours will still vary based on the amount of time you have and if you have other obligations like work and school.

When starting off with your LSAT preparation, choose a target test date that gives you adequate time to study. Based on the time you have available, you can design a study plan that allows you to live your life, but still be ready for the LSAT.

Without a plan, you're less likely to commit. You may end up basing your study on emotions and how you're feeling that day. Maybe you like Logic Games and don't touch Reading Comprehension for weeks because this is where you struggle.

I've integrated day-by-day study plans into my courses that show you exactly what to do. I've found this helps keep students from getting overwhelmed. To give you an example, if you're starting off with only two or three months until test day with no previous studying under your belt, your study timeline might first devote a few weeks to focusing on Games, then a few weeks to Logical Reasoning, and finally a few weeks to Reading Comprehension. After working on those individual question types and feeling comfortable with how well you are scoring, it's time to move on to timed individual sections. Once you know you are able to finish sections within the allotted time, you then build your endurance to take a full-timed exam. I'll include below a sample of how I structure my study plans, using Logic Games as an example.

I recommend that you initially focus on the Logic Games section. Start with Ordering games, beginning with the easy ones and working your way up to the more difficult ones. Next, work on Grouping games from easy to difficult, and so on with the other game types.

(As for how to learn about these game types, you get a brief introduction within this book, of course. For much more, my courses include live online classes via Zoom, along with on-demand video lessons covering each section and question-type in-depth. Visit lsatunplugged.com for more information.)

Once you've built a decent foundation in Logic Games, start completing individual sections, untimed. This will give you some practice completing a mix of different game types (just like on the real exam). Once you have a strong foundation in all sections and question types, start taking full-length timed exams.

If you are studying while working a full day or in school, you probably won't have enough time to do two exams a week, especially if you are doing them in the evening when you're most exhausted. If this is reminiscent of your schedule, just do one exam a week on the weekends and use the rest of the week for reviewing and drilling weak areas, along with trying out individually timed sections.

Maybe you do two practice tests a week if you're studying full-time, with at least one day in between, ideally two days. Doing one Saturday and one Wednesday would be an example of good spacing if your schedule allows.

If you're working on a shorter timeframe, it's wise to spend about two weeks focusing on Games, two weeks on Logical Reasoning, two weeks on Reading Comprehension, and two weeks on full-length timed exams leading up to exam day, all while developing your mindset and honing your thought process.

However, with any study plan you adopt, make sure you still mix in the other sections and question types while focusing a particular section to ensure that you don't get rusty. And don't wait just a week or two before Test Day to start taking timed sections and full-length exams; pacing and endurance are important!

Six to seven weeks before the exam

If you've already been studying for several months and have built a strong foundation, what do you do for the final six or seven weeks? **If you already have a strong foundation on the basics of the exam, I recommend you now work on pacing and endurance.** When you can, do a full-length exam, working to find an optimal pace. Then, on the other days of the week, do individual sections, 35 minutes timed, and do an excruciatingly detailed review of those sections and the full-length exams you did.

Two weeks before the exam

When you get to two weeks before your LSAT, if you have the time, I would say **two timed exams per week, along with detailed review** is ideal. If you can only do one timed exam per week, that's fine. On the other days, you can do some individual sections and review weak areas. If you're having trouble with particular Logical Reasoning question-types, for example, you can read chapters or watch videos on those types and maybe do a dozen or two dozen questions of that type afterwards. If you have particular trouble with science Reading Comprehension passages or grouping games, you can do some sections or questions involving that particular type, to drill it for extra practice, in addition to doing more exams.

At this point, however, your main focus should be taking and reviewing timed exams. Let's say there are 10 questions you got wrong and then 15 you guessed on. Even if you were lucky and got those questions correct, that's 25 questions to review right there. That could easily take three to four hours – or more – to review. I wouldn't recommend studying more than six hours a day, so that alone is almost a full day's worth of studying. Ultimately, you should have ideally taken at least 10 timed exams by test day, so that test day will be just another run-through for you.

However, if you're two weeks out and have not done close to 10 exams yet, don't worry. I wouldn't load them all up into the next two weeks. I would instead simply do two timed exams per week over the next two weeks to avoid overloading yourself.

If you have a full-time job and are unable to dedicate enough time per week to do two full-length, four-section exams and an adequate review of those exams, then I would recommend just doing a few sections, maybe two or three back-to-back, at least a few hours every week to stay fresh on the LSAT.

LASER approach

The LASER approach is the foundation of all my LSAT study plans. To recap my study plans, I recommend typically starting with Logic Games, because they are the most unfamiliar at first—they are the low-hanging fruit. Then we move on to Logical Reasoning while still staying fresh on Games. Finally, we add in Reading Comprehension, while still cycling in Games and Logical Reasoning.

This study plan framework will get you reach your fullest potential, but make sure to follow the steps in order.

L is for learning theory, which involves building your foundation and familiarizing yourself with the different question types, the different sections, and so on. You want to get an overview of what the exam involves, what Games are, what Reasoning is, etc. This involves reading books like this one, and reviewing my foundational course lessons first before jumping into questions. Any book or video should break down all sections, so you know what to do and what not to do. My video lessons go over the basics of the exam, step by step, bit by bit, in bite-sized pieces to make it more manageable.

A is for accuracy. Do individual questions by type, drilling them untimed to get used to what each type is asking for. For example, you should do 20 strengthen questions in a row, 20 weaken questions in a row, 30 grouping games in a row, etc. to start to see the patterns underlying each section and question type. When you open a book of full LSAT exams, you're seeing a scattered grab bag of questions without any rhyme or reason. In my courses, I unscramble them for you so you can approach them in a systematic fashion.

S is for sections. Do individual timed sections and start to develop your own pace. Figure out how best to allocate your time; for example, I'd recommend completing the easier Logical Reasoning questions faster, perhaps solving the first 10 in 10-12 minutes, so you have more time for the tougher questions that come later.

E is for endurance and exams. This process is doing full-length timed exams because, believe me, after two hours of the LSAT without much of a break, your brain is fried! On test day, the current format requires that you do two sections back-to-back. You're then given a short 10-minute break, then you do two more sections back-to-back. It can be grueling, so I'd recommend doing at least one timed exam per week in the final month or two before test day.

R is for review. Analyze where your mistakes come from: the stimulus, the question stem, the choices, something else? What is tempting about the wrong answer? What is discouraging about the right answer? Write this out, articulating it in some way, whether you're writing it out in a notebook, typing it out, or talking it over with a friend, study buddy, coach, or tutor. It's really important to get this out of your own head. When you're on your own, it's too easy to simply look at the correct answer and say, "I get it now," and move on. It is much tougher to articulate or paraphrase what the question says in your own words.

Can you articulate the major viewpoints presented in the passage of a Reading Comp passage or a Logical Reasoning question? Can you paraphrase the argument in your own words and explain it to somebody else, then talk over why it is the wrong answer? Can you explain why the right one is right? Can you reverse-engineer the exam to see it from the test makers' perspective and indicate exactly what was tempting in that wrong answer? What trap did LSAC lay? You need to be able to spot these.

If any one of these five things is missing from your preparation, it will hold you back, and you need to take a step back and focus on the particular issue. A lot of students jump straight to exams because they want to see the results. They do exam after exam, thinking they're reviewing, but they are not. This is inefficient and burns through valuable practice material. If you're not doing the kind of review where you're articulating your challenges, writing them out, looking for patterns in the unique tricks and traps that you're falling for, then you're not doing enough. You've got to integrate all of that into your prep.

Make sure you're going through this process in order. Only move on to subsequent steps after you have built the foundation by learning the basics of what the exam entails. If you simply do exams without learning the basics, it's like taking a diagnostic in a foreign language you've never studied. It's going to go worse than it otherwise could have because it is testing something you haven't learned yet.

Start with the easiest questions, such as simple ordering games, and move forward from there to harder material, like the toughest pattern or "curveball" Logic Games. If you've never covered the basics of grouping games, why would you do timed sections taht include grouping games? You don't know much of the material yet! Do the work untimed first. Focus on learning the theory, then the accuracy. Next, do the individual sections of that question type. Finally, complete full-length exams and review them.

Going from easy to hard within each category builds momentum and morale as you go, so you're not giving yourself anything too challenging too early. The LSAT is hard enough without studying in a way that discourages you.

3-step approach to studying for the LSAT

In the last section, I shared my five-step LASER approach. But what if you have less time to study? What if you'd like a more consolidated way to think about study plans? In this section, I share an abridged version of my framework.

Regardless of which approach you take, remember that blindly churning through exam after exam will burn you out, and you will have missed out on the great learning opportunities that each exam has to offer. If the exams you are practicing with are more recent, and therefore more valuable, you will have wasted your resources. **Designing an efficient study plan is essential to achieving your desired LSAT score.** Making your study program efficient means organizing it in a way that helps you learn the material effectively. The smart way to study is to plan out your prep in three phases: accuracy, pacing, and endurance.

Accuracy: In this step, you focus on untimed work. Accuracy means being able to get the right answer. It's not worth anything to say you got through the entire LSAT exam in record time if you didn't get a decent score. The first step is building a solid foundation, and that requires that you can get the right answers under untimed conditions. You can take as much time as you need on each question during this phase of study. Your goal is only to get the questions right, no matter how long it takes. This is your foundation, and it is essential if you want to master the next two phases.

Pacing: In this step, you focus on your timing with individual sections. Here, you are still solidifying you foundation, but it's time for you to pick up the pace so that you can complete each section within the time constraints you'll have on Test Day (35 minutes with standard timing).

Endurance: Last, but not least, step three brings it all together. Endurance will prepare you for test day. During this phase, you will work through a full-length timed test. I recommend sitting through at least five full-length timed exams to build your exam stamina. (Ideally, complete 10 before Test Day if you can.) Can you actually get through the exam and maintain the accuracy and pace you have worked on until now?

Improving accuracy

The first step in LSAT preparation is simply to answer the questions correctly. This is your foundation. Later, you can progress to the pacing and endurance stages. Using the most recent 10 exams is sufficient if you're on a short timeline, but working through 20 or 30 exams will be far more beneficial if you have the time. And, if you do, keep the 10 newest exams for strictly timed, full-length practice closer to Test Day and use the older ones to build your foundation.

I recommend working through the sections types in the following order:

Games – Work through the easier games first, like the ordering or sequencing games. Next, move onto the grouping games, starting with the easier ones and working your way towards the difficult ones. After this, there are combination games and curveballs, which I'd save for last since they are the most difficult and don't neatly fit into any category.

Logical Reasoning – Same idea here: start with the easier questions and work your way up. There are about a dozen types of questions in this category, but question-difficulty typically relates more to a question's position within a section than the particular question type. However, I would still recommend starting with questions in the "Inference" category before moving onto the other question-types.

Reading Comprehension – There is not a clear order of difficulty in terms of "passage types," so my advice is to just dive in. Some recommend reading The Economist or Scientific American. These have value, but the best source of practice material will always be actual passages from past LSAT exams. There are nearly 100 released LSATs, which means you have nearly 400 actual LSAT passages to study; why go beyond those?

Improving timing & pacing

Once you've worked on your untimed accuracy, it's time to work on individual timed sections to improve your pacing. Timing is especially crucial when working on Logical Reasoning because it's easy to get bogged down on the tougher questions. It's important to spot them and potentially flag them for later on, so you don't waste time.

Averaging eight minutes and 45 seconds per Logic Game or Reading Comprehension passage will allow you to complete all of them, but it's also wise to know which ones you can solve more quickly to allow more time for the harder ones. The LSAT has a strict time component, so working on your pace is essential. Maybe you can't hit the 35-minute mark yet. Maybe it takes you 40, 45, or even 50 minutes. But that's ok — everyone has to start somewhere. To challenge yourself, gradually reduce the time by a minute or two, until eventually you get to the target 35-minute mark.

Whatever you do, don't hold yourself to a hard and fast time constraint per question. Just make sure that by test day, you've done enough practice tests to have your own internal rhythm and pacing.

If you have a learning disability, don't panic over the time constraints. If you have a medical diagnosis for a disability that may hinder your ability to complete the LSAT in the allotted time, such as ADHD, you do have a valid case for accommodations. LSAC used to be overly restrictive, but they now give extra time to a good number of people. It is an enormous benefit, and it's definitely worth looking into if you believe you may qualify. However be aware that extra time will lengthen your test day to be several hours long, which can truly become exhausting.

Improving endurance

Once you feel comfortable with your level of accuracy and pacing, your next step is to bring it all together and work on endurance. Can you make it through a full exam without getting exhausted? This phase of preparation requires working through several full-length exams and simulating real-world test day conditions. For example,dDon't take practice tests on paper if you'll be taking the real one online.

REVIEWING TESTS

The importance of reviewing

A thorough review process requires painstaking detail. You're looking for the patterns in the tricks the test makers use, specifically the tricks you are susceptible to. You want to spot these patterns and be ready for them, so that you will select the correct choice next time.

Take Logical Reasoning, for instance. You want to look at where your misunderstanding stems from. Was it in the stimulus? Was it in the question stem? Or was it in the choices? If it was in the stimulus, was it about not properly understanding the conclusion versus the evidence, or the subsidiary conclusion, or the counterpremises? Or in the question stem, were you misinterpreting the question they were asking you to answer? And if the wrong answer choice was tempting, what made you pick or consider it? Ask yourself what ultimately made it wrong. How did they go about making their argument and what were you missing in their method of reasoning? What was discouraging about the right answer choice that pushed you away from it, and what ultimately made it correct?

A proper review of a single practice test can take at least three to four hours. Let's say you score really well and get a 170. A score of 170 means you got the vast majority of questions correct and only got a handful wrong. However, the ones you got wrong are not the only ones you should review. You may also have many other questions that gave you difficulty. Maybe you were down to two choices and you guessed and got lucky. Or maybe you got it right, but could have gotten it right more quickly. A few minutes per question is going to add up.

The reason you take practice exams is not simply to see how you'll do. It's not just to work on your pacing and endurance. Give yourself the opportunity to get questions wrong and then learn from those mistakes.

It should take much longer to review a question than it does to complete that question during the exam. At a minimum, you should spend five minutes reviewing each Logical Reasoning question, preferably more. You can look at explanations, but the real work comes from the review process itself, not from explanations. The work comes from engaging in your own critical thought process, which is why I'd rather you do fewer exams and go through them in more detail, than do a greater number just to measure your results.

In a perfect world, you'd want to review everything, wrong and right answers alike, but here's the issue: If you're doing 10 practice tests timed, that's about a thousand questions. You probably won't have time to review a thousand questions thoroughly in just a few months, and it's not necessarily productive to do so.

You have limited time and can only do so much. I'd rather you focus on the ones you got wrong or had difficulty with and leave it at that. You might find something you were unsure of (a particularly difficult game or passage). Perhaps you got three of them confidently right and four of them wrong and want to deepen your understanding. Maybe there's a game with a particular inference that would've let you solve it more efficiently. Maybe you could've made multiple main diagrams. Resolving these issues is painstaking work, but it's the best way to learn from your mistakes and improve for next time.

One thing you can do while working through your exams is **rate your confidence level on a scale of one to ten.** How confident are you in the choice you picked? This will help you remember whether you were certain about an answer you got right or guessed and got lucky. However, don't pick a middle-of-the-road number like six or seven. You want to be able to clearly know whether you were confident or you not.

The amount of time you spend reviewing each exam depends on several factors. In part, it will depend on how many questions you get wrong. I recommend spending at least five to ten minutes per question you get wrong. This process could take at least two to three hours, maybe even three to four hours, if you're really giving it your all.

While not strictly necessary, I do recommend writing by hand when you engage in your review. Write full paragraphs for every question you get wrong or have difficulty with. This increase your retention and engagement. Typing the letter "D" is no different than typing the letter "H" to your fingers, but when you write longhand, you're actually solidifying the concepts in your brain more deeply.

If your correct answer was a guess, that's still wrong in my view. It could've just as easily gone the other way. Take the time to review on your own, independent of any explanations. (However, if you're feeling stuck, I do have video explanations for the vast majority of LSAT PrepTests in my courses. I also have many written LSAT explanations available through my website.) But the majority of the work is going to come from doing the review on your own. That's where the pattern recognition and deeper understanding comes from.

When you get questions wrong or have difficulty with them, it's essential to recognize why you got them wrong. So, don't be afraid of getting questions wrong, because every question you get wrong or have difficulty with is an opportunity to learn something new. I'd rather you do hard questions and get them wrong, than do easier questions and get them right. It's not about ego. It's about gaining an understanding that will benefit you in the long run.

Most LSAT prep books don't tell you to take fewer exams and do more review. But they're wrong. That was one key realization for me: quality, not quantity. It was a big breakthrough for me when I realized I should focus my studying on analyzing the exam from the test-makers' perspective, not the perspective of the student trying to beat (or worse, argue with) the exam.

The test-makers lay all kinds of traps for the unwary student. They plant wrong answer choices that go down specific flawed logical pathways, like making a mistake when taking the contrapositive or creating an answer choice that is the polar opposite rather than the logical opposite. These traps have a pattern. As you work through questions and learn what these traps are, you will increase your ability to find them and work your way towards the correct answer more often. The types of tempting wrong answer choices repeat themselves in every LSAT exam, so studying the 10 most recent exams should give you plenty of material to hone your ability to identify traps and avoid them. If you want a score of 165 or 170+, you've got to think like the test makers and ask yourself what a 170+ scorer would be able to do. Which tricks would they be able to avoid? And how many practice tests would they complete?

The more questions you answer and the more practice tests you complete, the more likely you are to associate a particular trick or method of reasoning with one you've seen before. In short, the more exams you do, the more patterns you'll be exposed to, and the more tricks you'll be able to avoid.

Because there are so many flawed method of reasoning, you might only have 10 questions that exhibit a particular fallacy within the flaw question stem category. However, if you do all 10 in a row, you'll really solidify your understanding of that method of reasoning. Another strategy is to go through the abstract language in flaw answer choices. Even if the correct answer is A, you can further your understanding by going through B, C, D, and E.

Perhaps they use abstract words like "takes the consequent to be an antecedent" or something of that nature, referring to necessary and sufficient conditions. If you actually parse out what all that abstract terminology means, you will deepen your understanding of how flaws are described, how an ad hominem flaw might be described, or how a correlation-causation flaw might be described. That way, when you predict or pre-phase the flaw for yourself, you will immediately recognize it in the answer choices.

One big area to focus on is relatives versus absolutes, weak language versus strong language for necessary assumption or must-be-true questions. You want to gravitate toward more moderate language that's more likely to be correct than extreme language. Tempting wrong answers will use the exact same phrases as the argument, but they will be a little bit too strong to be correct.

You want to look carefully at the language of the question to detect any particular traps you are likely to fall for so you can avoid making those mistakes in the future. Make sure that you're doing enough different types of questions and not, say, ten exams and forty games and passages. There are nearly 100 released exams at the moment. Ideally, you'll have the opportunity to do at least twenty or thirty (some timed, some untimed) to sample a wide range and prepare yourself for the unexpected.

There are some complex, counter-intuitive, unexpected methods of reasoning out there, and it's tough to puzzle through them under timed conditions on test day. The LSAT really is a test of pattern recognition, meaning that you want to relate new questions to questions you've done before (even if only subconsciously). As the methods of reasoning get more complex, they show up less frequently. You need to complete a really large variety of LSAT questions in order to ensure you get multiple examples of the highest-difficulty methods.

What makes the LSAT easier for me than for a newbie is that I have done every exam out there multiple times. When I see a new question, I can automatically, subconsciously, relate it back to something I've done previously. I'm not reinventing the wheel or interpreting that method of reasoning for the first time.

Analyzing those questions on a deeper level is really important to solidify your understanding of a particular concept, of a particular general principle, or of a method of reasoning. Misunderstanding questions is a little less common, but it's easier to fix because the question stems repeat a lot so there's only so much variation in question stem types. But LSAC does get tricky sometimes with unfamiliar wording in question stems.

It's incredibly important to notice if you are consistently misidentifying a question type and don't fully understand what they're asking for. A common example I see is where students confuse necessary assumption and sufficient assumption questions. These are very different question types, asking for very different things. It's very important to know the difference so you can approach the question from the proper perspective. They both might use the words "assumption" or "assumes" in the question stem, but there are other indicator words in the questions (which I've covered earlier) that tell you which one you're dealing with. Knowing the difference is a quick win.

To reiterate, invest plenty of time in reviewing. You might say, "But that means I can't do three or four exams a week." So, don't. Maybe doing one or two exams a week is enough. Some individual sections will give you plenty to work on. Then, if you want, you can do untimed work. Identify particular trends in questions you're getting wrong, determining certain weak areas like strengthen questions or grouping games.

If you don't notice trends in the questions you're getting wrong, don't worry. If you already have a pretty good foundation in a section by this point, you may be getting questions wrong simply because they're hard. In that case, drill tough questions and keep reviewing.

How to review your LSAT results and learn from them

When reviewing, there are several steps you might take to look into what you did wrong and how to reach the correct answer. First, you look at the answer key and then start the search for related explanations. That's straightforward and easy. You might even say it's too easy. You'll read the explanation and think, "Yeah, I should have seen that," or "That makes sense," or "How could I have been so dumb?" As the saying goes, hindsight is 20/20.

A better exercise is to mark all the questions you missed—and, as I mentioned earlier, questions you had difficulty with—and work through them once more, untimed. The second time around, you might correctly answer questions you got wrong or miss questions you initially got right. You should now walk through each question and ask yourself why you chose your particular answer.

In my coaching, I require students to sit down and engage with the problems giving them the most trouble. A lot of times, people just want to look at the explanations or have me explain things. I prefer to have a dialogue with my students, which forces them to go through a specific thought process to clarify their understanding and build their confidence.

Doing well on the LSAT does not involve memorizing information. It's an exam of pattern recognition. Learning this pattern recognition does not happen overnight and certainly won't happen on test day. Developing the skills required for the LSAT take hours, days, and weeks of practice before exam day. You want to learn about contrapositives, chaining conditional statements, creating correct diagramming strategies for Logic Games, and clear note-taking for Reading Comp until it all becomes second nature.

In my early LSAT coaching days, the newest book of ten exams was numbered in the 30s. The 40s had not been released yet. So, I ended up working through the 30s over and over for many years. This meant working through the same Logic Games at least 30 to 40 times, some up to 100 times over just a few weeks. I found that, on some of the games, I would get a new insight or inference on the 20th, 30th, and even 50th time doing it. It's amazing that even after doing a question more than 20 times, there were still new insights to be gained. The same goes for the Logical Reasoning and Reading Comprehension questions, but these patterns are more readily apparent in the Logic Games sections.

LSAC goes to great lengths to insert easy-to-follow paths of reasoning towards the incorrect answer. Part of your preparation should involve identifying those incorrect paths so you can avoid them and use the right reasoning to get the correct answer.

For the questions you got wrong on a practice exam, look at how you reasoned to get the incorrect answer and figure out the path you should have taken to get to the correct one. **Try to determine the source of your misunderstanding.** Was it in the method of reasoning, in the stimulus, in the wording of the question, in the question stem and your interpretation, or in the answer choices? This exercise will prove invaluable in your practice, across all question types.

Work on articulating your review process; in other words, write or type your reasoning yourself. Keep mistakes in a journal or even talk them out with a friend, coach, tutor, or anyone else who can help you elaborate your reasoning, even if they have nothing much to offer.

Talk to your dog if you want to. The point is that by talking out loud, you are forcing yourself to articulate your method in your own words, ideally without even looking at the question, so you can make sure you thoroughly understand the argument, the passage, or whatever the case may be. Once you talk it out, look back at the question. Do you understand it now? Do not use explanations as a crutch—not even mine—but puzzle through things on your own instead.

Understanding your mistakes is the hardest part of prepping. You want to score yourself and move on. But reviewing the toughest problems is where true growth comes from, since it allows you to avoid making the same mistakes over and over again.

Evaluating answer choices

When it comes to evaluating the answer choices, this is typically where most students need to focus. You have tempting wrong answers and you have discouraging right answers. I like to imagine that when LSAC writes a question, they initially write at least two or three correct choices, then tweak a few to make them wrong. It might just be one little word change but, as you know, a little bit wrong is actually all wrong when it comes to logic. You've got to learn to distinguish that little tweak that made that answer choice wrong so you are able to spot it the next time.

Then, after eliminating the wrong answers, what remains may not seem perfect, and it may not be the way anyone normal would have worded it, but it's "the best of the worst" options and technically correct. You see this most often in Reading Comprehension, where the main point, primary purpose, or passage organization correct answer choices often aren't the way you would have worded them.

Of course, clear and concise is not LSAC's goal, so you've got to pick the best of the worst. That's why process of elimination is so important and useful, especially on LSAT Reading Comprehension.

I wrote this book to be **timeless**, but I also want to make sure you get access to the **most effective** and **up-to-date tactics and strategies**.

I regularly update **LSATUnplugged.com** with new techniques as I develop and discover them.

STUDY STRATEGIES

Strategies for answering tough questions

What's the best way to proceed when you encounter a dense Reading

Comprehension passage and you just can't make heads or tails of it? Should you skip it, or should you attempt it in the moment? If you're aiming for at least a 160, 165+, you're going to want to be doing all four passages, no question.

If you've already invested time in reading the passage, you've got to slow down and ask: "Can I walk away with simply the main point? What is the primary purpose of the passage? Why did the author write this?" If you can't walk away with that, you need to slow down. You have no hope of getting the questions right with no understanding of the passage. Find the main idea. Find the primary purpose. **Typically, there will be a key line or two where they summarize the main idea or the author expresses their opinions.** Look for that keyword or keyphrase.

If a game has you totally stumped, slow down and see if you can at least knock out the orientation question. That tells you how LSAC is thinking about the game and may give you an idea of how to diagram it. Next, your local questions will help you build up those previous valid scenarios and give you an immediate jump off point. Finally, do the tougher global ones and make use of all your previous work, as well as the correct answer for the orientation question.

If it's taking you too long to answer, move on. You do not want to get bogged down. It leads you to run out of time. If you feel like you're getting diminishing marginal returns, flag it, skip it, and trust that you will be able to come back to it later. And if you can't, that's okay, too. It's not the end of the world if you skip a tough question and instead getting your points on the easier ones. It's ultimately about what's going to get you the most questions correct in the end, and that involves cutting your losses sometimes.

You have to know your weak areas. Maybe it's a lengthy parallel reasoning question. Maybe it's a curveball Logic Game. Maybe it's a science-focused Reading Comprehension passage - whatever it is for you, focus there.

Common LSAT prep mistakes and how to correct them

Students also have a tendency to continue practicing things they're good at to try to make themselves feel better about the test. Their reasoning is, "If I just pass all the Reading Comprehension questions, then I can afford to fail on some Logical Reasoning." That's a fundamentally flawed way to look at the exam, because, at the end of the day, it's very unlikely that you will get all the questions of every section correct, even your best section.

Believe it or not, some students try to do Logic Games entirely in their heads, without diagramming. It pays to learn how to draw diagrams for Logic Games. One big reason being that you can draw hypothetical scenarios and reuse them for future questions. Any hypothetical scenario where you have laid out the variables, so long as it's in compliance with the rules, can be used to solve a more general question later.

For Reading Comprehension, a common mistake I see, is **spending far too long taking notes, underlining, circling, and highlighting.** This is, in my eyes, a big waste of time, because you might then only have 30 seconds per question associated with that passage.

Lastly, I see far too many students fail to prepare for the actual Test Day format. Taking practice tests with the online format and getting familiar with all the highlighting and underlining features, etc., ahead of time will help you focus more on understanding and answering the questions during the test.

Challenges with finding study time

Finding time to study can be a real challenge. It can make or break your success in getting the LSAT score you're aiming for. Some students work full-time, some part-time, some are in school, and some have family obligations.

So how do you carve out the time you need to succeed? You want to set a realistic timetable, taking into account work and school. It's all about balance. **Your first goal may be to study like it's a full-time job.** If you already have a full-time job, that will be a challenge. You may burn out if you are studying 40 hours a week on top of whatever else you're busy doing. Instead, treat your LSAT prep like a part-time job. Commit 10, 15, or maybe 20 hours a week to it and fit those hours into your schedule according to what's best for you. It could be four hours on Saturday morning and another four hours on Sunday morning. Right there you've got eight hours, and you haven't entirely disrupted your weekend.

If your weeknights are free, schedule some time then. A few hours each evening can help. If you are working a full-time or part-time job, maybe work out a temporary altered schedule for the weeks leading up to the exam so you can squeeze in more study time. If you work a 9-to-5 or 9-to-6 job, consider getting to work early to find a conference room and study for an hour or two before your workday starts. Maybe use your lunch hour to answer one or two questions or read articles.

Study time outside the house is more effective because you can focus without distraction. Let's be real: as soon as you get home and put on your PJs, you have Netflix, social media and other distractions. You're better off staying a little bit after work or finding a coffee shop nearby and studying for a few hours before you go home.

Another way to easily fit in some passive exam prep is to **watch videos or listen to podcasts during your commute to and from work or school.** I created the LSAT Unplugged YouTube channel and podcast for exactly this reason: to allow students to prepare for the LSAT when it's not possible to study using a book or computer. Once you're home, try to squeeze in an hour or two before or during dinner, depending on what works for you.

Once you are done for the day, completely unwind and relax. Your mind and body need to recuperate from the day so you can recharge and re-energize for the next day.

For those of you who are students or taking summer classes, consider LSAT prep like a six-credit class and fit in the hours you need in the space available throughout the week. Maybe you have a day that's light on class time, so use that free time for your LSAT. Block off LSAT prep time into your calendar so something else does not take over, especially on weekends and days you don't have classes. LSAT prep won't happen if you don't plan and commit to it.

The LSAT weighs more heavily in law school admissions than your undergraduate GPA, yet people typically don't devote as much time and effort to it as they do to their college classes. You may not have a lot of flexibility with your college class schedule, but the LSAT is important. **If possible, try to put your work and school obligations hold for the week or two leading up to the LSAT.** A lot of my students take off from work the week before – or, at the very least, the day before. If the exam is on a Monday, they take Friday off to relax a bit, maybe do another full-length timed exam. If you're in school, delay your assignments until after the LSAT if you can do so without letting your grades slip.

You should, ideally, be studying at least 15-20 hours a week. That is the minimum. Of course, you could do more, but you may run the risk of burnout. Your study schedule should include off days or breaks as well, so make sure you are taking those so you don't burn out or become overwhelmed.

Should you take practice exams the week of the actual exam? You certainly can. However, I would never recommend doing two full-length exams on consecutive days. It's a recipe for burnout.

Sometimes less is more. What you can do is perhaps take a full-length exam one day then spend the following day doing nothing but reviewing that exam.

I typically recommend a maximum of two exams per week, maybe three if you are studying full-time and have no other obligations. You could take an exam on Monday, review it on Tuesday, drill weak areas and foundational material on Wednesday, then repeat the cycle with a new exam on Thursday. The exams you take in the final month should be fairly recent (from the past few years).

When doing these exams, ask yourself what value are you hoping to get out of them. Another high score under your belt to help you feel confident? Or are you trying to cram out of fear that you have not done enough up to this point?

If you haven't done my recommended 10 full-length exams yet, don't try to squeeze them all in the one week before the exam. At this point, just be happy with whatever you've done. Sure, tf you can do another two, that's great. The value is really just in getting more under your belt in terms of pacing and endurance so that you're ready for that full-length experience on test day. I would rather you do fewer exams and review them in more depth, as it'll help you more on test day.

Write your own LSAT problems

The real insights that led my score increase from a 152 to a 175 finally came when I started seeing the exam from LSAC's point of view. Then I was able to dissect questions and look at how they were constructed. Instead of looking at the answers, I started thinking about how I would create my own LSAT questions. What would that process look like? What tricks would I use to tempt test-takers into a false sense of security and lure them down an incorrect pathway?

I learned more than ever about the LSAT when I started writing my own LSAT questions. I actually wrote seven or eight LSAT Logic Games on my own, which you can see on my website. It's a lot harder to write LSAT questions than you would think!

To level up your prep, I want you to think about how you might write your own LSAT problems, your own Logic Game, or even just a mini Logic Game drill. Maybe it's a tempting wrong answer for a Logical Reasoning question, or a discouraging additional right answer for a given Logical Reasoning or Reading Comprehension question. Note: this is a technique for those seeking top scores. Not everybody needs to do this, but it is really a useful exercise.

In particular, writing wrong answer choices is really hard. Sure, you could write an answer choice that nobody would ever pick, like saying the president of the United States is Homer Simpson. Crafting tempting wrong answer choices is especially important, because they're the ones you're most likely to pick.

I recently had a student in my courses write a couple of her own Logic Games. For the first game, she created four associated questions. Two were invalid, meaning there were multiple correct answers or no correct answers.

But I thought the second game she wrote was perfect. There were no mistakes at all, and it was actually tougher than I expected and took me more time than I would've thought! While it can be difficult to come up with games like this, it's not as difficult as you might think, and it's extremely helpful in teaching you to see the exam from the test-makers' perspective.

Strangely enough, there are plenty of books out there containing fake LSAT games with mistakes in them! As an exercise, once you've gotten fairly proficient in Logic Games, you might want to look at some of these books with fake LSAT questions and have fun spotting the mistakes. For example, take LSAT for Dummies. Quite frankly, it's a terrible book with lots of errors in the answer key and in the problems themselves. While that's not particularly useful for the typical student, it could be a good thing if you'd like to work through these games to look for their mistakes.

In the games I've written, my difficult questions lead you down paths to take advantage of the typical mistakes you might make. There's nothing more sneaky than leading someone to confidently choose a wrong answer and walk away feeling good about it. (This is often what the LSAT test-makers are doing as well!)

Personalized help

Does working with an expert help? If they are knowledgeable in their field and have been doing it a long time, they can absolutely be a great resource. Working with someone can be helpful if they're able to engage with your thought process and help you find gaps in your understanding and the way that you approach the problems.

Along with all the material I create, I still reserve the time to work with a small number of students in my courses because I understand the enormous benefit of learning from someone who's been through this process before. Regardless of who you might work with, be sure to get a sense of their experience and style first. You want to make sure it's a good fit.

Study groups can also be enormously helpful. Let's say you're scoring in the 140s and your study partners are in the 160s. You can help each other. The person who is scoring in the 160s has a better understanding of the LSAT and can give you advice. On the other hand, if you're the one in the 160s, it can help your understanding to explain it to someone else. It's extremely beneficial to discuss LSAT problems, as it forces you to articulate your own thought process and acknowledge your blind spots. Real growth comes from articulating it in your own words. If you're talking with someone who understands it better than you, they might point out gaps in your reasoning. They can show you where you did not understand something as fully as you could have.

If you're someone who learns best in a social environment, you may want to consider an LSAT course or study group. I offer live online LSAT classes that students can join from anywhere in the world, and my students often hold study groups. I also manage the LSAT Unplugged online community where students discuss the LSAT and law school application process, share study strategies, and ask questions. It can be a great asset during the study process to have a community of like-minded individuals.

Studying plateau

If you're at a plateau with your LSAT prep, it could mean you're burned out, in which case it's worth taking a break. Or maybe it's time for you to change your approach. If there's a resource you've been thinking about getting or using, it's time to make the investment. This could be a book, a course, coaching, or tutoring. Whatever it is, think about how to maximize your prep to bring it to the next level when you're stuck at a plateau. What are you missing? What could propel you to make a breakthrough in your understanding?

Whatever you're considering, whatever you think could help you, make the investment. Just a single additional point on the LSAT could lead to thousands of dollars more in scholarship money, getting into a better law school, or getting off a waitlist. This is why it's so important to take a break and come back refreshed. Then you can approach the LSAT from a different angle, push through that plateau, and further prepare yourself for test day.

Avoiding burnout

You must recuperate between intense periods of studying. Too many students, especially those studying full-time or those with few obligations, run the risk of burnout. You don't want to put in 6, 7, 8 hours a day. Typically, I recommend a maximum of 5 or 6 hours in a single day. Maybe study from 9 to 12, take a break for lunch, and then go on for another two or three hours. That's it.

As simple as it sounds, just keep your study time focused on studying. Don't have your phone open. Don't have your email handy. Don't have Instagram or TikTok easily accessible during study periods. It's better to just get your studying done than to go back and forth between a little bit of studying, a little bit of social media. This just drags out the process. You'll be more productive during your studying if you can trully focus, get it done for the day and be able to relax and socialize guilt-free.

If you want to feel like you're making progress in your LSAT studying, but just can't stand another minute of staring at practice questions, check out the LSAT Unplugged YouTube channel and podcast. (I do also have related TikTok and Instagram accounts – @LSATUnplugged.) These are useful tools to give you a break from doing questions, but still keep you moving forward.

Taking breaks

I definitely recommend taking days off from your LSAT studying. In fact, I build days off into my study plans because I understand that it's important to have that time to recharge. I'm also aware of the fact that life happens. You have work or college classes, or you have family obligations, or you have a vacation or holiday, or you get sick. Things come up. I build in buffers so you won't feel like you're falling behind constantly, and this is something you should definitely incorporate into your own study plan.

We all have things going on in our lives, but try not to let an entire week go by without studying. If your timeline is a span of two to three months, a day off here and there is fine; don't stress! If you are taking the LSAT next year, then you might want to take a more slow and steady approach, where you gradually study and build up as you go. Just don't forget to take days off to refresh and recharge.

Reducing LSAT stress

One thing you might want to do to reduce stress before your scheduled LSAT test date is to register for the next one. That way, you know you'll have a backup in case things don't go well during the test. Yes, it does cost an extra couple hundred dollars, but if it gives you peace of mind and you have the room in your budget, it's definitely worth it.

Or if you're not feeling ready before Test Day, you can always postpone or withdraw, and law schools will never even know you were registered in the first place.

Remember that the LSAT is now offered nearly every month, so it's easier than ever before to retake. And the nice thing about retaking the LSAT is that you only have to stay fresh on the material for another 4-8 weeks. Considering the value of getting just a point or two more by retaking (or waiting), it's well worth the investment.

Finally, I can't overstate the importance of resting the day before your exam. Use the time to relax and recharge, because you will likely still feel jitters on test day. A day or two off from studying before Test Day can help to get you into a good mental space before you sit down and take the test. No matter how much you've prepared, it can still be a shock when that timer starts going when you know it's the real thing. But remember that if you've done several long runs already in the months leading up to that final moment. It's not really that different. It's all mental. Because you've done it before, you can do it again.

TEST DAY PREP

First, I want to share a story about my own LSAT test experience, something I don't think I've actually shared before. On the morning of the LSAT, I was nervous, as is to be expected. I had read that it's good to eat protein because it's brain food, so I had a bagel with a can of tuna fish on it. I'd woken up at around six in the morning and subjected my stomach to this brutal breakfast within 20 minutes.

Needless to say, it did not go well. About five minutes after eating that bagel, I got nauseous. I went to the bathroom and threw the whole thing up. I was sweating and nervous and even more panicked about the test because of what I'd just put my body through.

On the road to the test center at Pace University, downtown Manhattan, I stopped at a fruit stand. I grabbed a banana, and that was all I ate. I had recovered by that point and took my exam as planned. I ended up getting my 175, so that just goes to show you that you can still score well despite test day issues!

Know that if you face an obstacle on the morning of the exam, you can still overcome it. You can still pull all your knowledge, experience, and strategies together and surpass whatever comes your way. If I had to do it over, I would certainly do that part differently. I recommend eating a lighter protein—not a full can of tuna fish! Maybe pilot what you are going to eat a few mornings prior for possible digestive or other issues. Suppose you generally drink coffee at exactly 8:00 AM, and it takes you 30 minutes to finish it. How will it impact you? I'm not trying to stress you out, but I would suggest playing around with time to find what works best for you. Also, consider that coffee is a diuretic. You don't want to have to go to the bathroom at the start of section two, because that is going to cost you time.

Let's say you're taking the exam on a Saturday. You might want to do a dry run on Tuesday or Wednesday if you can, or even do a full-length exam and eat the exact same breakfast planned for test day the weekend prior as an experiment. Try to keep all other aspects of that morning as similar as possible. Hopefully, you can avoid what I experienced on my LSAT test day!

Now, let's get to the typical questions. **One question I'm often asked is how to avoid the dreaded test day drop.** If you're not familiar with the test day drop, it's when someone is scoring around a particular range in the leadup to the exam, and then, for one reason or another, they end up scoring at least a few points below their expected score range.

There are a number of reasons this can happen. Among them are nerves, anxiety, and not having simulated test day conditions properly. That can involve anything from not being ready for distractions like noise and movement, to not being prepared to have certain sections in a particular order, such as having two Logic Games sections back-to-back.

The remedy is to take practice tests that mimic these exact possibilities. Whatever you're most afraid of is the scenario you should simulate.

Some lower-than-expected scores relate to anxiety. One technique to mitigate this is mindfulness meditation—even just five minutes focusing on your breath can make an enormous difference. If you start doing it early on, it can have an even greater impact, giving you the focus to remain calm and collected.

LSAT test day is not the time to try new strategies you haven't attempted before. Stick to what you've done on the practice exams in the lead-up to test day. If you want to test a new strategy, do it a week or two before the exam to see how it works for you. Stick to what you know and what you've practiced.

Managing time while taking the test

Remember that every question is worth the same number of points. There's no sense getting bogged down in a tough question if there may be an easier question later. After studying and teaching this exam for several years, I've gotten to the point where I have a time bank of around five minutes for any questions left at the end.

How do you build up that time bank? You blast through the easy questions. You do not second guess yourself on thems. When you encounter a difficult question in Logical Reasoning (for example, parallel, a principal-application or a question involving abstract language), just skip it if you don't want to deal with it in the moment. Use your time bank to come back to it at the end.

LSAT SCORES

When you'll get them and how to read them

Unfortunately, you don't get your LSAT scores instantly. LSAC does detailed statistical analyses to measure the results and compare student performance with their expectations, which can take between two to three weeks. LSAC's said they hope to release results faster in the future. (Fingers crossed!)

Would it be possible to get your score back immediately at some point in the future? Certainly. Or at the very least, they could give a raw score calculation of how many questions you got right. (I'm not holding my breath on this!)

But LSAC is very careful, deliberate, and scientific about how they do things, and they want to allow themselves a few weeks to make sure that the questions are performing as anticipated with the testing population. As such, count on the timeline for score releases being approximately three weeks. If you get your score back sooner, it'll be a nice surprise.

Fluctuating scores

An issue of concern I often see is fluctuating scores. Someone might get a perfect score on Games their first time then only half right on the next test. Why does this happen? What can you do to get your score more steady, reliable, or consistent? **Score fluctuations are incredibly common.** Nothing is ever perfectly consistent. There is a margin of error of three and a half points on each end—a seven-point band. This means you could get a 161 one day and a 167 the next, and theLSAT is still considered valid! Work on your ability to remain calm and collected, even if you're being thrown for a loop.

Standardized tests are not perfect. However, the LSAT is reliable and relatively consistent. The same person will most likely not get 171 one day and a 150 the following day. However, you shouldn't expect to get the exact same score every single time. There is always variation. One exam could have easier games, and the next may have harder games. If you're good at games, this will affect your performance accordingly. Additionally, you might not like a certain Reading Comp passage or understand it as well as you understand others, and that could also affect your performance.

All these factors put together lead to a certain degree of chance. Even if a 163 is your perfect ideal average, you won't get exactly 163 every single time. You might do three and a half points lower, or three and a half points higher—where that seven-point band comes in.

Therefore, if you deserve a 165, you might get as high as a 169, or as low as a 161, or anywhere in between.

How to improve your score

What if you are scoring 165 now and aiming for 170? If you're consistently at a 165, you're likely at a plateau. The question is, what will you do between now and your test date to make that five-point increase happen? What haven't you been doing now? You need a breakthrough.

What could you incorporate into your prep? What could you be doing differently? Integrate those changes into your prep. Depending on where you're struggling, experiment with changes in terms of strategy and theory. See how these new approaches work for you, then adopt them or not.

I guarantee there is something you could be doing differently between now and test day that will close that gap. The key is figuring out what it is. I do not know your specific situation, but, in my experience, most people are taking too many exams and not spending enough time reviewing.

Many people get their score back and say, "Law school isn't for me," or they compromise and go to a lower-tier school. It comes down to spending more time—generally five or six months—to reach your fullest potential. I was average and thought I deserved a higher score. I was driven and obsessed with getting a higher score to prove to myself and others that I could get into a top 14 law school. To get there, I stopped simply taking tests and quickly checking the answer key and moving on. I became more deeply focused on my problem areas and mistakes. I saw that there were patterns on the test, and that I could learn to spot those patterns to avoid making the same mistakes in the future.

Take basketball as an example. You have one player who attempts 100 free throws without working on technique, and you have another who records himself shooting ten free throws, then watches himself back before shooting again. Who do you think will sink the most shots? It's the same for test taking. You can't prevail without doing the deep work of understanding what you were doing wrong and what you were doing right.

How to cope with a low score

Don't let your early low scores deter you from achieving a top score and going to law school. You can improve, and I am here as evidence. Based on my decade of experience helping students master the LSAT, I have one key piece of advice: You may get a lot of negative feedback from your practice tests and feel as if you're not good enough. A low practice score is harmful to one's self-worth. To push through, know that **you are not your LSAT score**, and you're certainly not your starting LSAT diagnostic score.

The LSAT is learnable. Aside from my own score improvement, I also I document the success stories of former students on my website. Many started in the 140s, but ultimately achieved scores in the 160s and 170s on Test Day. You can improve by 10 or 20 points or even more from wherever you're starting! Sure, it may take more than a month or two, but you can get there in the end.

So how do you deal with failure or disappointment? Regardless of wherever you score, remember that it's totally fine to retake the LSAT, and law schools only consider the highest score. Practice healthy lifestyle habits such as sleep, diet, exercise, relaxation, and mindfulness meditation. Be sure to make time for these habits and practices every day if possible.

If you got a low LSAT score

If you're stressed after getting a low score on Test Day, I just recommend adding an addendum to your application to let the admission officer know if there was something going on in your life that negatively affected your score. Then, retake and get a higher score!

Of course, many test takers are worried about law schools seeing their lower scores. Some fear this may be perceived negatively. Strangely, it doesn't matter if you did poorly a few times; what matters is that you did great in the end. Also remember that scores older than five years will be removed from your record, meaning law schools will not see them.

If you were to get 155 three times consecutively, chances are that's where you stand and it's not going to change change much unless you radically change your approach to LSAT studying before retaking. But, if you were to take the exam a fourth time and you got 170, that's a score that law schools could use to help them increase their standing in the U.S. News rankings, which would give them incentive to ignore the previous run of 155s. (Schools rank better when they admit students with higher scores.)

I recently heard from someone in Canada who said, "Unlike the U.S, our schools take the highest score." Well, it turns out law schools in the U.S. take the highest score, too! It's important to realize that there might be some outdated information out there, even on law schools' websites! Schools also want to give the appearance of being holistic—it just sounds nicer. Remember that schools have strong incentives to focus on the highest scores given the importance so many place on the U.S. News rankings, which use the highest scores of schools' matriculating students.

(Obviously, it's better to have a single 170 than to have 170 either preceded by or followed by a 160. But it doesn't matter whether the 160 came before or after the 170. The 170 is what matters.)

Impact of LSAT scores on admissions

If your LSAT score is above the median of a school to which you are applying, that school has extra incentive to admit you, because, if you choose to go there, you will raise their median a bit. If they do that with 20 or 50 applicants, it could actually have a significant impact on their ranking. They may also give you a significant discount on tuition to attract you to choose their school over another. If your LSAT score is high enough, you could get a full ride and pay nothing!

Which law school you decide to go to is ultimately a personal decision. If you get a 175 and have a solid GPA (above 3.5), you could reasonably go to any top 14 law school. If you're looking at a school ranked 50th, you'd be far above their median with 175. Some people would say you'd be crazy to choose that school.

But if you could go to law school for free and graduate without debt, would you do it?

Not everybody would, but for some who want to stay local, it might be a reasonable course of action. What most people don't know is that the majority of law students are not paying the sticker price for tuition. This is why LSAT scores are worth real money.

LSAC has a LSAT/GPA calculator on their website where you can input your undergraduate GPA and your actual or predicted LSAT score. It will show a graph of how you compare to each law school's LSAT and GPA medians, which serves as a rough estimate of your chances. Obviously, numbers aren't everything, but they can be a good indicator of your chances since law school admissions process is largely numbers-driven, unlike undergraduate admissions.

If you're still in college, focus on getting straight As for now if necessary; you can always come back to the LSAT later. But the truth is that even if you're a junior or senior, there's not as much you can do about your GPA at this point relative to getting a higher LSAT score. Your previous grades are what they are, and you can only move your overall GPA so much with any future classes that you take. If you're already out of college, GPA pretty much a done deal since your LSAC-calculated GPA doesn't factor in graduate school classes.

Your LSAT score will always remain the biggest way to improve your chances of law school admission, as well as scholarship money. Getting a higher LSAT score is the easiest money you'll ever make.

But while your LSAT score is important in the admissions process, it's not an indication of how you'll do as an attorney. Being a successful lawyer involves people skills, networking abilities, business acumen, and much more. There are plenty of people who got low LSAT scores and went to low-ranked or even unranked law schools who still had very successful careers based on the networks they were able to build. The LSAT is correlated with first-year law school grades, but it won't determine your entire career.

Is it better to withdraw or cancel?

After the test, you'll first feel relieved that it's all over, but then you'll likely start to wonder about the result. The first question that may come to mind is, "Should I cancel this test score?"

You have up to six calendar days to decide whether to keep or cancel your score. Sure, you could cancel that day, but I wouldn't recommend it, because you may be making a rash decision. When you're at the peak of your stress after spending a few hours taking a difficult exam, you may not be able to make the most clearheaded decision. And since you have several days, why rush the decision? There's no downside to waiting a few days until you can evaluate the decision more calmly and rationally.

Because you don't get your score right away, you typically won't know what your score is when making the decision to cancel (unless you're a first-time test-taker using the "Score Preview" option).

You will be deciding whether to cancel solely on your memory and feelings about of how the exam went. That's why I never suggest canceling unless:

(1) you know for a fact that something went terribly wrong during the exam, e.g. you skipped a whole game when normally you complete all four games, or there was a major tech disruption.

(2) you were never scoring close to your goal score on practice tests. For instance, if you're aiming to attend a top 14 law school but you were consistently

scoring below a 160 on your practice tests, that kind of score probably won't put you in the running, and there's not much reason to keep it.

However, if there's any chance it could be a score you'd want to apply with, i.e. a score that will boost your chances of admission to the schools you want to attend, you might as well keep your score on record to be on the safe side. You can always retake the LSAT in the future if necessary.

Alternatively, if you took the LSAT and feel pretty good about it, even if you think you could do better the next time around, you may want to keep the score. Even if you plan to take the LSAT in the future, something may come up in your life – work, family, school, etc. – that interferes with your studying or even prevents you from retaking the test.

Prior to 2006, law schools averaged all LSAT scores on record when making admissions decisions, so canceling made perfect sense for many. However, the American Bar Association changed their policy in 2006 to require law schools to report only the highest scores of their matriculating students. In turn, U.S. News started considering only wanted the highest scores for rankings purposes. However, LSAC still gives you the ability to still cancel a score, even though it doesn't actually provide much real benefit (other than the peace of mind to be able to hide what might be a low score).

With the LSAT being offered almost every month, students are retaking it more often than ever before. However, it's important to properly prepare before each take. Law schools can see all takes on your record, and LSAC does limit the number of times you can take the LSAT, so you want to time your test dates appropriately and only sit for the exam if you feel you are ready.

A sidenote on LSAT retake limits: you can take the LSAT three times in one cycle, five times in a five-year period, and seven times over the course of your life. Once you get a 180, you can't take it again. Those upper limits are really more for folks like me. If all the professional tutors and instructors took the exam over and over again, they might screw up the so-called curve. LSAC does not want to skew their test-equating process. They also want to limit the number of times applicants could potentially see the same test content from one administration to another, which would, of course, taint the validity of the exam. (They reuse exams because it's extremely expensive to create new test content, and they must administer multiple test forms for each administration.)

The best way to avoid the dilemma of when to cancel and how many times to retake is to really assess if you are ready to take the LSAT. Before you do, calculate the evaluate the average score you've gotten on your five most recent practice tests. If it's not close to what you want, postpone (if the deadline has not yet passed) or withdraw. There will be no trace that you registered and withdrew.

That's right — law schools will never even know that you were registered for the exam. I highly recommend this course of action if you are not ready. The last thing you want to do is go through the stress of taking the exam only to cancel. It's important to note that canceling too many scores may not reflect well on you when you apply to law school. While cancellations show on your record and count towards LSAT retake limits, withdrawals (and postponements) do not.

RETAKING THE LSAT

The LSAT is currently offered nine or ten times per year (nearly every month!), a big jump from the previous four times a year. This gives you more options and opportunities to take and retake the exam. It also means shorter time periods between exams, so if want to retake the LSAT on the next scheduled exam date, you'll typically only need to study for another month or two.

If you do a timed exam per week, along with a detailed review of each exam, that alone could be enough for your LSAT retake prep. If you additionally focus on improving your weak areas, you could do even better. By taking the exam more times, you increase your chances of getting a higher score; for that reason alone, it's worth trying.

A lot of students ask me whether they should write an addendum if their score wasn't as high as it could have been, or if they had a tech issue with the LSAT that caused their score to be lower than expected. The answer is generally no. Just retake to get a higher score. Law schools understand that tech and proctoring issues will happen. They're certainly aware of these issues, but don't let them become an excuse. Simply retake the test. Admission officers see plenty of people retaking multiple times. There's nothing wrong with that.

For some reason, the myth persists that taking the LSAT multiple times looks bad. But that is not the case. Taking it two, three, or four times is worth it if it allows you to increase your chances of achieving a higher score.

As you begin your retake prep, ask yourself what can you do differently the next time around with regard to your study schedule. If your work schedule is packed or your class schedule is full, maybe you can reduce those workloads a bit.

Then there is the question of whether you had the right resources, and whether you used them to the fullest possible extent. Maybe you didn't buy enough real exams or didn't do enough of them. This is something you can easily change in the future. If you can improve your study plan and increase the amount of studying you did, then retaking is well worth it.

A retake after a month doesn't necessarily require a ton of extra work if you already have a strong foundation, but know that it doesn't pay to be a perfectionist. Do what you can and move on with your life. It's like polishing the same 500-word essay for years and years and years to little avail. You can obsess over every word choice, editing and re-editing, but at a certain point, you have to decide that it is good enough.

Prepping for a retake

Many students are concerned about reusing old material when studying for a retake. Say you've burned through many recent exams and don't know what to use now. What if you've already done every LSAT PrepTest ever? I get emails from students all the time saying, "I have done every single LSAT PrepTest ever released. What do I do now?" Students in this position often feel like they can't use that exam again. However, I always ask them, "Well, are you perfect at everything? So you think you'd get a perfect 180 if you took that very same exam again?"

The answer is probably no. Why? Why couldn't you get a perfect 180 if you've attempted all the questions before, reviewed them in-depth, and seen all the correct answers? Because there's still more that you can learn from that exam! If you have seen the same question and correct answer several times but are still getting it wrong, there is something missing. Either there's a gap in your understanding, or something about the incorrect answers keeps tempting you toward picking them.

The LSAT is really hard and no one has a perfect memory. That means you're actually prone to making the same mistakes over and over again. If this is happening to you, it means you did not review enough to solidify your understanding of the concepts that messed you up on your first or second attempt. That's why, despite having done those practice exams already, you can benefit from reviewing those questions again.

With that being said, if it's your first time taking the LSAT and you are aware that you might need to retake it in the future, save some new exams. For example, you might want to do every recent even-numbered exam in the lead up to first your test date, then save all the odd-numbered exams for a potential future retake.

I always laugh when people say, "I can't do the same exam again." Of course you can! There's always more to learn from exams. I still get value out of reviewing exams, and I've done the same questions hundreds of times with students. When you read or watch my explanations, they are not necessarily realistic representations of what you need to be thinking in the moment as you complete a problem. As I've mentioned, when you are redoing problems it's important that you don't only look at the ones you got wrong. You want to look at those where you weren't sure, or the ones where you guessed and got lucky. Next time, you might not be so lucky, so make sure you are looking at every question you had even a slight difficulty with.

There are thousands and thousands of tricks the LSAT test makers use. You're most likely not falling for all of them, or you would be getting every question wrong!. You want to identify which of those tricks you are uniquely prone to falling for so that you can avoid falling for them in the future. If you've done every LSAT ever released and think you have a solid understanding of the exam, you could try to write your own LSAT questions, your own game, or your own Reading Comp passage, just to have a different perspective of the exam and see it from the test makers' perspective. When I created my own LSAT problems, it really helped me see and appreciate the exam for what it is.

LAW SCHOOL ADMISSIONS EXTRAS

Soft factors to keep in mind for your application

In addition to the LSAT, law schools also consider soft factors like your personal statement and letters of recommendation, but they are not nearly as important. You do want to show that you're mature and have fully considered the investment. You must convey the reasons why you want to go to law school. My most important advice: forget all the media portrayals of courtroom battles when writing your personal statement. Sure, they are glamorous and inspiring, but they don't really reflect what lawyers actually do, which is lots of paperwork!

Working as a paralegal or another source of direct exposure with the law is great material for your personal statement, but avoid telling a sob story or writing a laundry list of every single thing you have done.

Instead, one common approach to focus on a particular experience would be starting with an anecdote about what you did during an internship and go on to show how it impacted your desire to go to law school. Whatever you do, don't try to mimic legalese; you haven't gone to law school yet. Admission officers don't want to read an essay that's written like a contract. Stick with a normal writing style.

You want to be absolutely sure that you make your essay specific to their school and why you want to attend their particular law program. You could name particular classes, professors, electives, or extracurricular activities. If you have visited the law school campus or have met alumni, be sure to mention that. Show any familiarity you have with the specific school.

These essays are usually limited to a few double-spaced typed pages. Be sure to proofread your rough drafts. If they are too long, now is the time to cut them down. You can have friends, family, professors, a coach, or a tutor review them. If you aren't feeling 100% confident in your application, I also offer admissions essay editing that covers everything from the personal statement to character and fitness disclosures. Lawyers should be diligent and double and triple check things, so it's important to demonstrate your capabilities now. Look over your personal statement ten, twenty, even a hunderd times if you must. Be sure it is a coherent narrative. You want it to be as polished and professional as possible.

Many students are reluctant to have others read their essays, but feedback from others is an invaluable tool. If each person gives you one comment, it could transform your personal statement altogether. Reach out to people on LinkedIn who are alums of the law school you're targeting. Email them saying, "Hey, can you look at my personal statement?" Believe it or not, they likely will. That can be a huge help. You can also go the route of hiring an editor or admissions consultant, which I highly recommend, whether that person is me or someone else.

Be honest in the character and fitness portion. If they ask if you've ever been arrested or convicted, disclose it. Include any disciplinary action in college if the questions requie it. If you lie or fail to disclose anything (lie of omission arer still lies), you may have a big problem when going before the bar to get a license to practice law. You wouldn't want to invest three years of your life in law school but never get to practice due to some silly failure to disclose on your application.

For your letters of recommendation, it is best to choose a professor and/or employer. Two or three letters is pretty standard. Request them early, from people who actually know you and have seen your work. Don't use your cousin's friend who is a judge or anyone you met at a coffee shop or cocktail party. Don't try to get a letter from a congressperson or judge unless you know them extremely well. Admission officers don't care about their fancy title. They want someone who knows you personally and is able to evaluate you well. Ideally, they've supervised you in some way or graded your papers or exams.

You could even supply your recommenders with a couple of reminders of particulars like a work initiative, term paper, or project. Professors often have many other students asking for recommendation letters for graduate programs, fellowships, and the like, so be sure to give them ample time. Maybe there's a professor you had a few years ago and you have to remind him or her who you are. Quick tip: it is always good to stay in touch with these people over time, even once or twice a year, just to stay on their radar.

All good writing takes time, so you should aim to get your application materials done early, and request your recommendation letters early.

With your LSAT prep as your focus and your law school application essays and recommendation also on your radar, you'll have all you need to have the best possible chance at getting into the law school of your choice.

Study smart, put your best foot forward, and know that I'm always just a click away for all of your LSAT needs.

Get instant access to the free
Easy LSAT Cheat Sheet I've created for
you at **LSATUnplugged.com**.

Made in United States
Orlando, FL
24 August 2023

36379350R00068